DISNEP · PIXAR

Story Collection

5 Stories

2

길벗스쿨

Disney·Pixar Story Collection 2

초판 발행 · 2022년 11월 22일 | **발행인** · 이종원 | **발행처** · 길벗스쿨

주소 · 서울시 마포구 월드컵로 10길 56(서교동) | **대표 전화** · 02)332-0931 | **팩스** · 02) 323-0586

홈페이지 · www.gilbutschool.co.kr | **이메일** · gilbutschool@gilbut.co.kr

기획 및 책임편집 · 이경희(natura@gilbut.co.kr), 한슬기, 임채원 | **디자인** · 이현숙 | **제작** · 이준호, 손일순, 이진혁

영업마케팅 · 김진성, 박선경 | **웹마케팅** · 박달님, 권은나 | **영업관리** · 정경화 | **독자지원** · 윤정아, 최희창

한글 번역 · 최주연 | **영문 감수** · Ryan P. Lagace | **전산편집** · 연디자인 | **녹음** · YR미디어 | **CTP 출력 및 인쇄** · 교보피앤비 | **제본** · 경문제책

▸ 잘못 만든 책은 구입한 서점에서 바꿔 드립니다.

▸ 이 책은 저작권법에 따라 보호받는 저작물이므로 무단전재와 무단복제를 금합니다.
  이 책의 전부 또는 일부를 이용하려면 반드시 사전에 저작권자와 길벗스쿨의 서면 동의를 받아야 합니다.

ISBN 979-11-6406-449-6 64740 (길벗 도서번호 30516)
     979-11-6406-447-2 64740 (세트)

정가 22,000원

제 품 명 : Disney·Pixar Story Collection 2
제조사명 : 길벗스쿨
제조국명 : 대한민국
전화번호 : 02-332-0931
주　　소 : 서울시 마포구 월드컵로
          10길 56 (서교동)
제조년월 : 판권에 별도 표기
사용연령 : **8세 이상**
KC마크는 이 제품이 공통안전기준에
적합하였음을 의미합니다.

CONTENTS

Disney · PIXAR
Story Collection 2

COMPONENTS

Main Book

5 popular stories based on Disney movies

인기 많은 디즈니 애니메이션 영화 5편의 내용을 한 권에 담은 콜렉션입니다. 영화 장면을 생동감 있게 표현한 일러스트와 오리지널 스토리를 가장 충실하게 녹여낸 문장으로, 원서 읽는 즐거움뿐만 아니라 영어 실력까지 향상시킬 수 있습니다.

Characters & Key Words

알아두면 원서 읽기가 쉬워지는 단어들을 선별했습니다. 등장인물들의 이름 표기와 맥락 이해에 중요한 역할을 하는 키워드 40개를 학습해 보세요.

캐릭터

키워드

MP3 Audio Files

QR코드를 스캔하면 아래의 음원을 들으면서 학습할 수 있습니다. 스트리밍 듣기 또는 전체 파일 다운로드가 가능합니다.

🔊 Key Words
📖 Story Reading

바로 듣기

길벗스쿨 e클래스

eclass.gilbut.co.kr → 학습 자료실

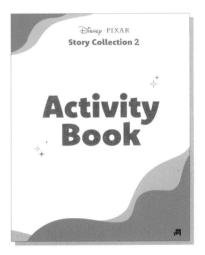

Activity Book
Includes book quizzes, questions for words, sentences, details and reading skills

스토리를 읽고 나서 얼마나 잘 이해했는지 진단하는 북 퀴즈를 제공합니다. 15개의 문제를 풀어 보고, 맞힌 개수를 확인해 보세요.
액티비티 파트에서는 다양한 유형의 연습문제를 접하며 단어, 문장 구성, 세부적인 내용 이해뿐만 아니라 글의 전체 구조까지 파악하는 힘을 기를 수 있습니다.

Word Check

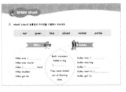

Story Check

Sentence Check

Story Map

Practice Book
for words & sentences practice

어휘력과 문장력을 강화하는 연습용 워크북이 제공됩니다. 각 장면에 등장하는 어휘의 철자와 뜻을 정확히 익히는 단어 연습장과 빈칸을 채워 문장을 완성하는 문장 완성 연습장으로 이뤄집니다. 문장 완성 연습장은 본책 스토리의 우리말 뜻을 확인하는 해석본으로 사용할 수 있습니다.

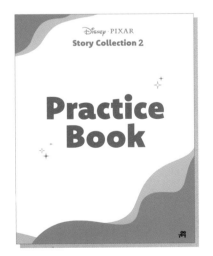

Word Practice

Sentence Practice

HOW TO READ

∞ 영어 실력이 한 단계 업그레이드 되는 원서 읽기 ∞

Step 1. 워밍업, 키워드 살펴보기

책을 읽기 전, 내용 파악에 핵심적인 역할을 하는 단어들을 미리 살펴보세요. 스토리에 등장하는 주요 캐릭터들의 이름을 확인하고, 내용을 예측해 봅니다.

Step 2. 집중 듣기

손으로 단어를 짚어가면서 원어민 성우의 음성을 귀 기울여 들어 보세요. 이런 집중 듣기를 통해 낯선 단어가 어떻게 발음되는지 정확하게 알 수 있으며, 음원의 속도에 맞추어 눈으로 읽어 내려가는 연습을 하다 보면 많은 양의 글을 빠르고 정확하게 읽을 수 있는 능력이 길러집니다.

Step 3. 소리 내어 읽기

소리 내어 읽어 보세요. 소리 내어 읽을 때 눈으로 보는 텍스트와 귀로 듣는 소리가 연계가 되고, 반복하여 읽을수록 읽는 속도와 정확성이 향상됩니다. 이런 과정에서 단어와 문장 구조를 인지할 수 있고, 뜻을 기억해내며 독해력을 발달시킬 수 있습니다.

Step 4. 북퀴즈로 이해도 확인하기

스토리의 내용을 얼마나 파악했는지 북퀴즈를 풀어 점검해 보세요. 맞힌 개수가 적다면 스토리북을 꼼꼼히 다시 읽으면서 정확히 이해할 수 있도록 합니다.

Step 5. 워크북 학습하기

Activity Book을 풀이하며 스토리의 세부내용을 살펴보고, 스토리에 담긴 영어 표현과 문장 구조를 익히는 시간을 가져 보세요.
또한 Practice Book을 통해 어려웠던 단어나 의미를 분명히 알지 못했던 단어를 별도로 학습하며 어휘력을 높이고, 문장 하나 하나의 정확한 의미를 확인해 보세요.

Characters

Elsa

Anna

Christoff

Olaf

Hans

Key Words

☐ kingdom	명 왕국		☐ memory	명 기억
☐ magical	형 마법의		☐ caution	통 경고를 주다
☐ create	통 만들어내다		☐ fear	통 ~를 두려워하다 명 두려움
☐ delighted	형 아주 즐거워하는		☐ control	통 조절하다, 통제하다
☐ accidentally	부 우연히, 실수로		☐ glove	명 장갑
☐ hurt	통 다치게 하다 (hurt-hurt-hurt)		☐ lonelier	형 더 외로운 (lonely의 비교급)
☐ rush	통 서둘러 보내다		☐ terrified	형 무서워하는
☐ mystical	형 신비한		☐ without	전 ~없이
☐ cure	통 치유하다		☐ gather	통 모으다
☐ change	통 바꾸다		☐ courage	명 용기

Key Words

☐ crown	통 왕관을 씌우다 명 왕관		☐ palace	명 궁전	
☐ marry	통 결혼하다		☐ beg	통 애원하다	
☐ forbade	forbid(금지하다)의 과거형		☐ frozen	형 얼어붙은	
☐ pull off	~을 벗기다		☐ spell	명 주문, 마법	
☐ expose	통 드러내다, 노출시키다		☐ advise	통 충고하다, 조언하다	
☐ flee	통 도망치다		☐ thaw	통 녹이다	
☐ fault	명 잘못		☐ refuse	통 거절하다	
☐ reveal	통 (비밀 등을) 드러내다		☐ danger	명 위험	
☐ led	lead(이끌다)의 과거형, 과거분사		☐ save	통 구하다	
☐ hire	통 고용하다		☐ melt	통 녹다, 녹이다	

Disney

FROZEN

Illustrated by GRACE LEE,

MASSIMILIANO NARCISO, and

Written by VICTORIA SAXON

ANDREA CAGOL

Designed by TONY FEJERAN

Not long ago in the kingdom of ARENDELLE, summer had arrived!

But it was winter inside the castle where
Princesses ᛖLSA and ᗩNNA were playing. Elsa
had **magical powers** and could create things
out of snow and ice! She made a snowman
named Olaf. Anna was delighted.

Then Elsa accidentally hurt Anna.

The king and queen rushed both girls
to the mystical trolls in the mountains.

The trolls cured Anna by **CHANGING HER MEMORIES** of Elsa's magic. They cautioned that others would fear Elsa's power. To help her control it, Elsa's parents gave her gloves.

With the castle gates closed, Elsa stayed away from Anna—she never wanted to hurt her again. But

Elsa missed ANNA.

Anna missed ELSA.

16

Years later, the king and queen were lost at sea. Without their parents, both princesses grew **LONELIER** and **LONELIER**.

Soon it was time for Elsa to take over as QUEEN. She was terrified that without her gloves, she might lose control of her powers in front of everyone!

Anna, on the other hand, was excited to meet new people—especially a prince named Hans.

THEY FELL IN LOVE!

Elsa gathered all her courage to take off her
gloves—and was successfully crowned Queen
of Arendelle!

With her gloves back on, Elsa proudly stood before her people.

But when Anna told Elsa that she wanted to marry Hans, Elsa forbade it. How could Anna want to marry a man she had only just met?

Frustrated, Anna tried to stop her sister and accidentally **PULLED OFF** one glove.

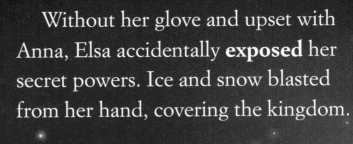

Without her glove and upset with Anna, Elsa accidentally **exposed** her secret powers. Ice and snow blasted from her hand, covering the kingdom.

Fearing she might hurt someone and ruin her kingdom,
ELSA FLED.

Anna thought it was her fault Elsa's powers had been revealed. She rushed off to find her sister.

She hired a mountain man named Kristoff to be her guide.

In time, Anna and Kristoff found a snowman
named Olaf. He was alive!

Anna **REMEMBERED** him—and the
good times she had shared with her sister.
Olaf led the way to Elsa.

Elsa was enjoying her time alone.

Now she was free to create whatever she wanted.

24

She built an ICE PALACE.

Anna begged Elsa to go home
to thaw her frozen kingdom.
But Elsa feared she couldn't
control her powers.

Angry and afraid, Elsa accidentally cast a
magic **freezing spell** on her little sister . . .

. . . and then created a **GIANT SNOWMAN**.
Anna and Kristoff ran. Olaf ran, too!

Anna's hair began to turn white. Kristoff led her to the trolls for help.

The trolls advised, "Only an act of **TRUE LOVE** can thaw a frozen heart."

Anna needed Hans for a true love's kiss!

Quickly, Kristoff and Anna headed back to Arendelle.

When Anna found Hans, he **REFUSED** to kiss her. His plan all along had been to take over the kingdom. Anna was crushed!

Anna realized that Kristoff loved her!

She needed all her strength to find him.

Meanwhile, Elsa had returned
to Arendelle to save her kingdom.
But now she was in **TERRIBLE
DANGER**.

When Anna saw Hans, she knew
what she had to do.

Anna
SAVED
Elsa.

It was an act of true love—true love
BETWEEN TWO SISTERS.

Soon the ice melted. And Anna realized she was in love with Kristoff. As for Elsa, she became queen again—a good queen who had learned from her sister that LOVE was the key to controlling her powers.

Characters

Nemo

Marlin

Dory

Key Words

☐ above	젠 ~위에		☐ caught	catch(잡다)의 과거형, 과거분사
☐ underwater	튀 물속에		☐ save	동 구하다
☐ scared	형 무서워하는		☐ disappear	동 사라지다
☐ spotted	형 점무늬가 있는		☐ give up	포기하다
☐ striped	형 줄무늬가 있는		☐ look for	~을 찾다
☐ sneak	동 살금살금 가다		☐ bump	동 부딪치다
☐ deep	형 깊은		☐ silly	형 어리석은
☐ embarrass	동 당황하게 만들다		☐ remember	동 기억하다
☐ surface	명 수면, 표면		☐ thought	think(생각하다)의 과거형, 과거분사
☐ ocean	명 바다, 대양		☐ search	동 찾아보다 명 검색

Key Words

☐ belong	동 ~에 속하다	☐ escape	동 탈출하다
☐ diver	명 잠수부	☐ fish tank	명 수조
☐ attach	동 붙이다, 달다	☐ trap	동 가두다 명 덫
☐ mean	형 못된	☐ pride	명 자랑스러움, 자부심
☐ address	명 주소	☐ brave	형 용감한
☐ repeat	동 반복하다	☐ swallow	동 삼키다
☐ shape	명 모양	☐ harbor	명 항구
☐ point	동 가리키다	☐ grab	동 움켜잡다, 붙잡다
☐ ride	명 타기 동 타다	☐ overjoy	동 매우 기쁘게 하다
☐ spread	동 퍼지다, 퍼뜨리다 (spread - spread - spread)	☐ return	동 돌아오다

Adapted by Victoria Saxon

Illustrated by Scott Tilley

Designed by Disney's Global Design Group

Now, most of you who are reading this book probably live above the sea…

…but others live underwater

Nemo and his father, Marlin, lived underwater. They were clownfish.

Because they were clownfish, they were small. But other fish were big!

Marlin was scared of the big fish, so he always kept Nemo close to him, tucked safely inside their little home.

But today was Nemo's first day of school!
He was very excited. On the way there he saw...

a **s p o t t e d** fish...

...and a **striped** fish.

He saw *angry* fish . . .

. . . and

H$_A$PPY fish.

Mr. Ray, the science teacher, took
Nemo's class on a field trip. Nemo
and his friends sneaked away and
swam to the really deep water.
Marlin chased after Nemo and
scolded him! Nemo was angry that
his father had embarrassed him in
front of his new friends…

...so he swam

...and swam

...and swam

way up to the surface
of the ocean until he
touched a boat!

45

Then Nemo got caught!
"Daddy!" cried Nemo.
"Nemo!" cried Marlin.

Nemo was taken away in the boat. Marlin
tried to save his son, but the boat sped away
so fast it soon disappeared. Nemo was gone.
But Marlin would not give up. The only thing
on his mind now was finding Nemo.

Looking for help, Marlin swam into all sorts of fish. They pushed him and shoved him. They bumped into him. Soon Marlin was knocked aside.

One friendly fish named Dory swam down to
see if Marlin was okay. She was a little bit silly,
and she couldn't remember very much, but
she was happy to help Marlin!

Together, Dory and Marlin met a shark. Marlin was scared! But Dory thought it was very nice of the shark to invite them to a party.

The party was for sharks who were trying not to eat fish. Luckily, they did not eat Marlin and Dory.

Marlin kept searching for
Nemo. He and Dory found a
scuba mask that belonged to the
diver who had taken Nemo. They
swam down into a very deep,
dark place to get it.

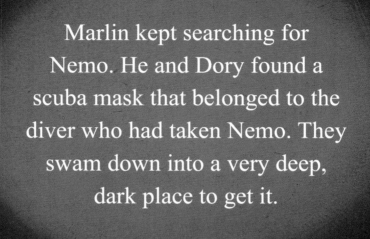

Then they saw a light.

The light was attached to a mean anglerfish! But it helped Dory read an address written on the mask. Then the two friends swam away before the anglerfish could eat them! Now Marlin knew where to find Nemo: 42 Wallaby Way, Sydney. Dory was so excited that she repeated the address over and over... and over.

Next Marlin and Dory met some moonfish.
The moonfish made funny shapes.

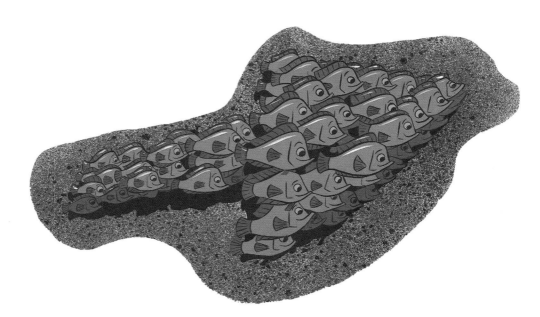

They pointed toward 42 WALLABY WAY, SYDNEY

Some friendly
turtles gave Marlin and Dory a ride.

Marlin told the
story of his search
for Nemo, and the
news spread across
the ocean!

Even Nemo heard about it at 42 Wallaby Way, Sydney. He was very excited! He wanted to escape from the fish tank where he was trapped.

Nemo's new friends were excited, too. The little
clownfish was bursting with pride. He had the bravest
dad in the sea!

Then a whale swallowed Marlin and Dory!
Dory told Marlin he didn't need to worry.
    And she was right. The whale took them
as close as he could get to 42 Wallaby Way,
Sydney. In fact, he took them all the way to

Sydney Harbor!

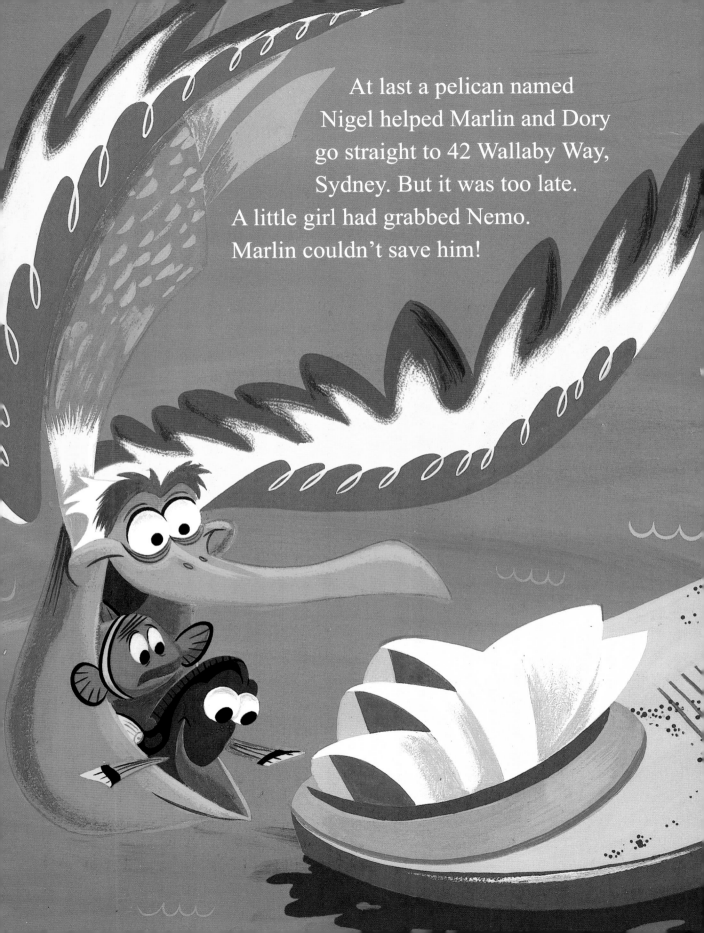

At last a pelican named
Nigel helped Marlin and Dory
go straight to 42 Wallaby Way,
Sydney. But it was too late.
A little girl had grabbed Nemo.
Marlin couldn't save him!

Marlin was sad. He thought he would never see his son again.

But Nemo had escaped! Dory found him.

Father and son were overjoyed.

And when they finally returned home, both Nemo
and Marlin were heroes.

Mike

Sulley

Oozma Kappas

Key Words

☐ scary	형 무서운	
☐ scare	동 겁주다 명 겁주기, 놀람	
☐ university	명 대학	
☐ serious	형 진지한	
☐ except	전 ~을 제외하고	
☐ lazy	형 게으른	
☐ prove	동 입증하다	
☐ matter	동 문제되다	
☐ fail	동 (시험에) 떨어지다	
☐ kick	동 발로 차다	

☐ compete	동 경쟁하다
☐ join	동 가입하다, 합류하다
☐ roar	동 으르렁거리다
☐ least	부 가장 덜 (little의 최상급)
☐ campus	명 교정, 캠퍼스
☐ underground	부 지하에
☐ try	동 시도하다
☐ beat	동 이기다
☐ rest	명 나머지
☐ cheat	동 속이다, 부정행위를 하다

Key Words

☐ librarian	명 사서	☐ flat	형 납작한
☐ argue	동 다투다, 언쟁을 하다	☐ ceiling	명 천장
☐ distract	동 주의를 돌리다	☐ practice	동 연습하다
☐ grab	동 붙잡다	☐ setting	명 설정, 무대
☐ realize	동 깨닫다	☐ thrilled	형 아주 신이 난
☐ pay off	성과를 올리다	☐ scream	명 비명 동 비명을 지르다
☐ eliminate	동 탈락시키다	☐ mad	형 매우 화가 난
☐ pretend	동 ~인 척하다	☐ forbidden	형 금지된
☐ vanish	동 사라지다	☐ enormous	형 막대한, 거대한
☐ background	명 배경	☐ powerful	형 강력한

Disney · PIXAR
Monsters
UNIVERSITY

ADAPTED BY
TENNANT REDBANK

ILLUSTRATED BY
MATT CRUICKSHANK

DESIGNED BY
STUART SMITH

Mike was small. And green. And round. Some monsters would say he wasn't very scary. But Mike had plans, **BIG** plans. Someday he was going to be the greatest Scarer the world had ever seen!

And the first step? Learning how to scare at Monsters University!

Mike was a serious student. He liked
studying. He liked his classes. In fact, he liked
everything about school ... **except Sulley**.

Sulley was another student in Mike's Scaring class.
Mike and Sulley just didn't get along. Mike thought Sulley
was lazy. Sulley thought Mike was too little and cute to be
scary. Mike couldn't wait to prove Sulley wrong!

Mike **WORKED** hard.

Sulley
played.

Mike
STUDIED.

Sulley went to
parties.

Mike got **A**s.
Sulley got **C**s.

But it didn't matter.
During a big test, Mike and
Sulley got into a fight. Both
monsters failed!

Sulley and Mike were kicked out of Scaring class. How would they become great Scarers now?

Mike wasn't ready to give up his dream. He saw a poster for the Scare Games. Winning the Scare Games would prove he was scary. Then the university would have to let him back into Scaring class!

There was one catch. To compete in the games, Mike had to join one of the school's teams.

The Roar Omega Roars didn't think Mike was scary enough to be a member of their team. But the Oozma Kappas liked him. With Mike, the Oozma Kappas had five monsters. They needed six to be in the games. Did anyone else want to join?

Sulley did! He wanted to get back into Scaring class, too!

But how could the Oozma Kappas ever win the Scare Games? They were the least scary monsters on campus.

ART

TERRI AND TERRY

DON

SQUISHY

Only Sulley looked like a **REAL** Scarer ...

BIG!

HAIRY!

SCARY!

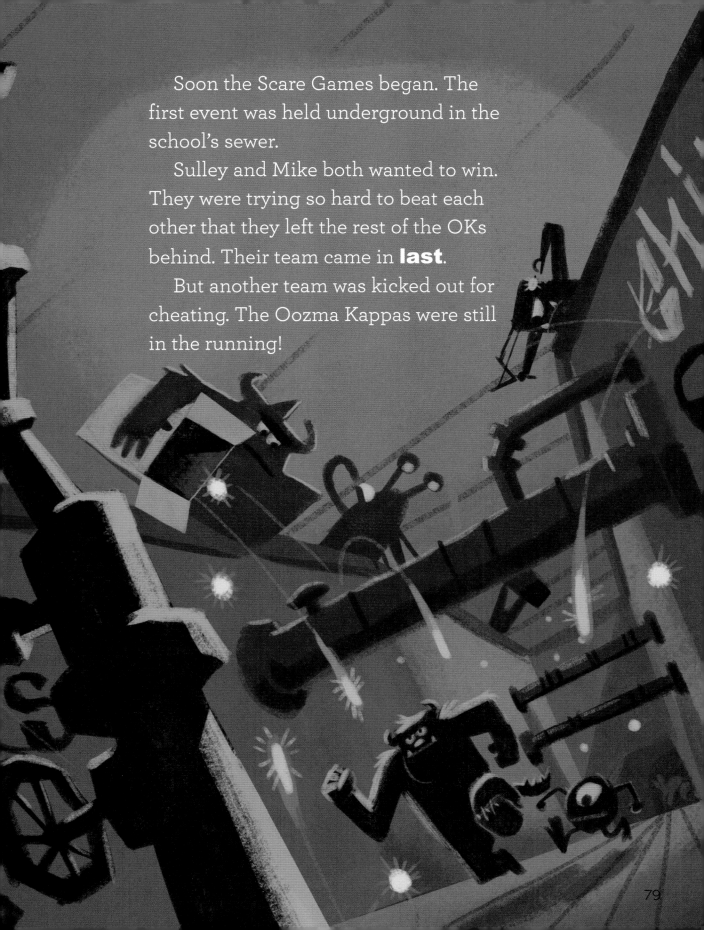

Soon the Scare Games began. The first event was held underground in the school's sewer.

Sulley and Mike both wanted to win. They were trying so hard to beat each other that they left the rest of the OKs behind. Their team came in **last**.

But another team was kicked out for cheating. The Oozma Kappas were still in the running!

For the second event, the monsters needed to sneak past the librarian to get their flag. While Mike and Sulley argued about the best way to win, the other Oozma Kappas worked together. Don, Terri, Terry, and Art distracted the librarian while Squishy grabbed the flag!

After that, Mike realized that if they worked as a team, they'd have a better chance of winning.

But Sulley didn't believe the Oozma Kappas could ever be scary enough to win the Scare Games. So Mike took them on a field trip to **Monsters, Inc**. The greatest Scarers in the world worked there—and they looked nothing alike!

Sulley realized there wasn't just one way to be scary.

The Oozma Kappas were coming together as a team. And their hard work paid off. One by one, the other teams were getting eliminated from the Scare Games—and the Oozma Kappas were doing better than ever!

In the Hide-and-Sneak event, Sulley pretended to
be a rug. Mike nearly vanished into the background.
But the star was Don. He stuck himself flat against
the ceiling!

Finally only two teams were left—the RORs and the OKs. The last event? **SCARING!**

The night before, Mike and Sulley practiced and practiced. Still, Sulley was worried. Was Mike scary enough?

Sulley wasn't taking any chances. He changed the
settings in the scare room to make it easier for Mike.
Mike was thrilled to get a huge scream in the event.
Then he found out that Sulley had cheated!

Mike was **MAD**. After all this time, Sulley still
didn't believe in him.

Mike decided to show everyone how scary he was. He'd scare a REAL child. He snuck through a forbidden door and into the human world. He found himself in a room of campers. Mike tried out his best scare— **"ROAR!"**
But the kids just smiled.

Sulley was sorry for cheating—and he was worried about Mike. Humans were dangerous! So Sulley followed him. But they both got trapped in the human world. Only one thing could get them out—an enormous scream. It would make enough energy to open the door back to Monsters University!

Together, Mike and Sulley came up with a plan that would **SCARE** the pants off the camp rangers.

Using scream energy from the scare, they found their way back to the monster world.

Mike and Sulley hadn't liked each other when they first met. But now they were **friends**. And they made a powerful team. They knew that whatever happened next, they'd be okay— as long as they stuck together.

Characters

Mirabel

Abuela Alma

Bruno

Isabela

Key Words

☐ wilderness	몡 황무지	☐ future	몡 미래
☐ glow	통 빛나다	☐ vision	몡 환상, 예지력
☐ communicate	통 의사소통 하다	☐ cave	몡 동굴
☐ knob	몡 (문·서랍에 달린) 손잡이	☐ destroy	통 파괴하다
☐ gift	몡 재능; 선물	☐ ripple	통 잔물결을 이루다
☐ heal	통 치유하다	☐ discover	통 발견하다
☐ worthy	혱 가치가 있는	☐ passageway	몡 복도, 통로
☐ crack	통 금이 가다	☐ restore	통 회복시키다, 복구하다
☐ shake	통 흔들리다, 흔들다	☐ doomed	혱 불운한
☐ prove	통 입증하다	☐ pursue	통 뒤쫓다, 추적하다

Key Words

- [ ] chaos   명 혼란
- [ ] embrace   통 포옹하다
- [ ] disrupt   통 방해하다
- [ ] revelation   명 드러냄, 폭로
- [ ] appear   통 나타나다, 발생하다
- [ ] fade   통 점점 희미해지다
- [ ] crumble   통 무너지다
- [ ] rubble   명 돌무더기
- [ ] entire   형 전체의
- [ ] wander   통 거닐다

- [ ] riverbank   명 강둑
- [ ] pray   통 기도하다
- [ ] push   통 밀치다
- [ ] protect   통 보호하다
- [ ] triplets   명 세 쌍둥이
- [ ] miracle   명 기적
- [ ] flame   명 불길
- [ ] important   형 중요한
- [ ] proudly   부 자랑스럽게
- [ ] rebuild   통 다시 세우다

DISNEP
ENCANTO

Adapted by
Naibe Reynoso

Illustrated by
Alejandro Mesa

Designed by
Tony Fejeran

In a small village deep in the wilderness, an ever-glowing candle shone brightly.

Its magic was so powerful, a place of wonder was born . . . an Encanto!

The Madrigal family lived there in a home they called Casita.

The magic blessed all the Madrigals with **special gifts**.

Julieta could heal people with food.

Luisa had **superstrength**.

Isabela could make flowers grow.

Antonio could communicate with animals.

And Bruno could see the future.
But nobody talked about Bruno. He had been gone for
many years.

When Mirabel was five years old, she got to wear her **special party dress!** She and Abuela Alma were so excited to find out what her gift was!

But when Mirabel touched the knob of her glowing door . . .
the magic went away!

She was the only Madrigal without a gift. This made her feel like she wasn't special enough or worthy enough.

One day, when Mirabel was fifteen, Casita started to crack.

It began to shake.

"The house is in danger!" Mirabel cried.
Suddenly, she had an idea. If she found the reason
for the cracks, she could fix them and prove she was special!

Mirabel followed the cracks straight to the magical candle. Her sister Luisa told her that Bruno left the Encanto because of what he saw in his last vision about the future. Could it have something to do with the cracks?

Mirabel was determined to find Bruno's vision cave.

After climbing endless stairs, she was finally inside his room. There, she found glowing pieces of his broken vision.

Mirabel put all the pieces of Bruno's vision together. The puzzle revealed a destroyed Casita, and in the middle was MIRABEL!

What did it mean?

Meanwhile, more cracks started to ripple through the house. Mirabel was running out of time!

She discovered a secret passageway inside the walls. And there she found . . . Bruno! He had been living there the whole while!

Mirabel asked Bruno to look into the future. She believed it would help stop the cracks and restore Casita's magic!

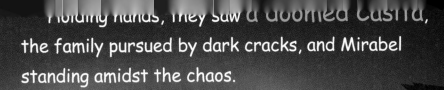

Holding hands, They saw a doomed Casita, the family pursued by dark cracks, and Mirabel standing amidst the chaos.

Then . . . a glowing figure . . . it was ISABELA!

"Embrace her and you will see the way," said Bruno.

Mirabel thought Isabela was annoyingly perfect. But Isabela told her that she always felt she could never be perfect enough for Abuela.

Just then, the candle's light glowed brighter!

Abuela Alma was angry at all that Mirabel had been disrupting. She told Mirabel that the magic had started dying the day she didn't get a gift.

Mirabel had a revelation: The magic was dying because no one in the family was ever good enough for Abuela Alma!

Giant cracks appeared everywhere! The candle was almost completely melted away. The family members raced to save the candle, but their powers were fading.

In its last effort, Casita got Mirabel to safety.

Then

poooofff · · ·

The candle went out.

All the magic of Casita was gone!

Casita had crumbled into a pile of rubble and dust.
The entire Encanto shook. Everything was in chaos.

Feeling defeated, Mirabel ran away.

Mirabel wandered past the
mountains. At a nearby riverbank,
Abuela found her. It was the same place
where the Encanto was born and
Abuelo Pedro, Abuela's husband, was lost.

Abuela told Mirabel about that night long ago, how she
had prayed for a miracle. The candle's bright light
pushed back the bad men, protecting her and her triplets.

Losing Abuelo broke something inside Abuela that no magic flame could ever repair.

Since that day, Abuela felt that if the family was strong enough and worked hard enough, she could protect them. But now she realized her broken heart had made her live in fear.

"We were given a miracle because of you," Mirabel told Abuela. This made Abuela feel better. "Mi vida . . . you are the miracle," she told her granddaughter.

Bruno arrived at the river. Abuela hugged him. "I feel like I missed something important," he said.

"Come on," Mirabel said, and the three of them headed home.

Nobody could believe what they saw: Abuela, proudly walking alongside Mirabel and Bruno! Everyone realized what made them truly special wasn't their powers, it was their family bond—their love for one another.

They all worked together to rebuild Casita. There was just one last piece of the house left: the doorknob. As Mirabel placed it in the house . . .

WHOOSH!

Casita came back to life, and the Encanto's magic was restored. The family's gifts worked again!

And at last, Mirabel felt her OWN worth and her family's love.

Characters

Luca

Alberto

Giulia

Ercole

Massimo

Key Words

☐ herd	동 (동물을) 몰다	☐ fascinate	동 마음을 사로잡다
☐ above	전 ~보다 위에	☐ soar	동 날아오르다
☐ surface	명 수면, 표면	☐ seaside	명 해변
☐ forbidden	형 금지된	☐ unsure	형 의심스러워하는, 확신하지 못하는
☐ warn	동 주의를 주다, 경고하다	☐ fisherman	명 어부
☐ collect	동 수집하다	☐ fee	명 요금
☐ treasure	명 보물	☐ fishy	형 수상한
☐ hide	동 숨기다, 감추다	☐ compete	동 경쟁하다, 참가하다
☐ transform	동 바뀌다, 변형시키다	☐ taunt	동 조롱하다
☐ hideout	명 비밀 은신처	☐ defeat	동 패배시키다

Key Words

☐ practice	통 연습하다	☐ suit	명 (특정한 활동 때 입는) 옷
☐ amazed	형 놀란	☐ complete	통 완료하다, 끝마치다
☐ reveal	통 (비밀 등을) 드러내다	☐ zoom	통 (아주 빨리) 휭 하고 가다
☐ shocked	형 충격을 받은	☐ trouble	명 곤란, 골칫거리
☐ threw	throw(던지다)의 과거형	☐ rescue	통 구출하다 명 구출
☐ harpoon	명 작살	☐ crash	통 충돌하다
☐ danger	명 위험	☐ injured	형 부상을 입은
☐ promise	통 약속하다	☐ bought	buy(사다)의 과거형, 과거분사
☐ risky	형 위험한	☐ accept	통 받아들이다, 수락하다
☐ identity	명 정체, 신분	☐ friendship	명 우정

Adapted by	Illustrated by	Designed by
Courtney Carbone	**Francesca Risoldi**	**Tony Fejeran**

Luca was a friendly sea monster who lived with his family in the ocean. He spent his days herding a flock of goatfish.

Though he dreamed about life above the surface, Luca was **forbidden to go on land**. His parents warned him that humans were dangerous.

One day, Luca met **Alberto**, another young sea monster. As Alberto collected some new treasures, he accidentally took Luca's shepherding crook.
Luca **chased him** all the way to the surface!

When they reached land, Luca and Alberto **transformed into humans**! Everything around Luca was strange but amazing.

Then Alberto took Luca to his **hideout.** It was full of neat human things, including a poster of a shiny **Vespa.** Luca was fascinated.

Looking around, he realized they could **build their own Vespa!** The boys got to work right away.

Every day on the island, Luca and Alberto made all
kinds of Vespas with anything they could find. They
even rode one together and soared through the air!
Luca had never had so much fun.

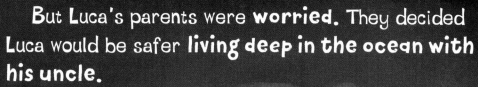

But Luca's parents were **worried.** They decided Luca would be safer **living deep** in the ocean with his uncle.

Before they could send him away, Luca left to find Alberto.

Luca and Alberto swam to the seaside town of
Portorosso, where they met a human girl named **Giulia.**
    She was unsure about the boys at first, but she soon
realized that they would be perfect teammates for a
local race called the **Portorosso Cup.** With the prize
money, they could buy a real **Vespa**—and then
they could go anywhere!

The boys met Giulia's dad, Massimo, who was a
fisherman. They agreed to work for him in exchange for
the race's entry fee. Massimo's cat, Machiavelli, kept
a close eye on the boys. He smelled something fishy!

Luca and Alberto knew that winning wasn't going to be easy. **Ercole**, the five-time race champion, was also competing. The bully **taunted the three friends** and vowed to defeat them.

More determined than ever, the team began training for the **three events** of the Portorosso Cup.

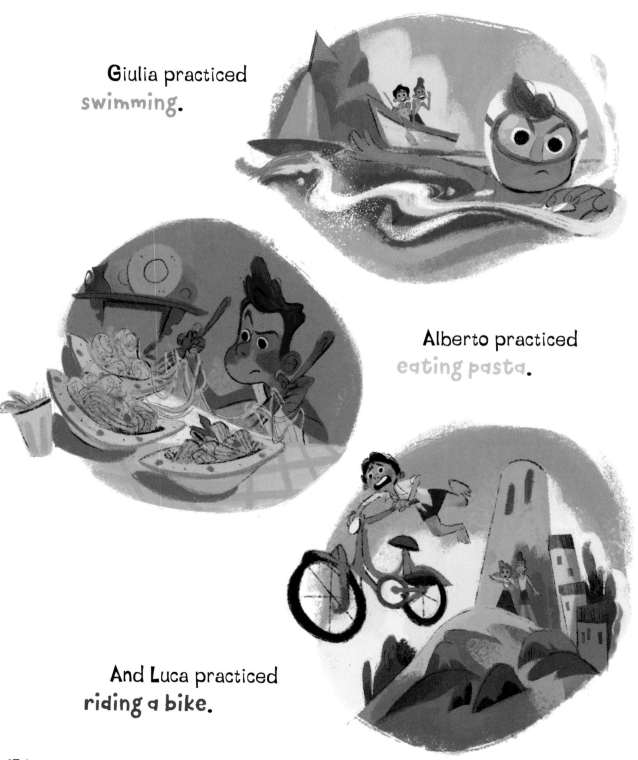

Giulia practiced **swimming**.

Alberto practiced **eating pasta**.

And Luca practiced **riding a bike**.

Over time, they became **good friends.**
Giulia and Luca loved to read and learn.

Luca was amazed that Giulia went to school.
He wanted to go, too!

Alberto began to feel left out. He didn't want Luca to go to school with Giulia, so he revealed that he was a sea monster! **Giulia was shocked,** but Luca stayed quiet.

Hearing the commotion, Ercole ran up and **threw his harpoon.** Alberto escaped just in time.

Giulia soon figured out that Luca was a sea monster, too. She was worried that Luca would be in danger if anyone knew the truth about him.

Later, Luca found Alberto. He was angry at Luca and didn't want to race anymore. But Luca wouldn't give up. He promised to get them a Vespa.

Finally, the day of the Portorosso Cup arrived. Luca decided to race alone to protect Giulia. It was risky to hide his sea monster identity.

During the first event, he wore a **diving suit** to avoid transforming in the water.

Next, he **completed** the pasta-eating competition.

During the bike race, Luca **zoomed ahead**, passing racers left and right.

He ran into his parents, who had been searching for him. But Luca kept pedaling as hard as he could.

It began to rain. Alberto arrived to help Luca, but he got into trouble: the rain transformed him into a sea monster! A crowd trapped Alberto in a net.

Luca rode into the rain and **rescued his friend.**
Now everyone knew Luca was a sea monster, too! The
boys raced away as Ercole chased them.

Before Ercole could take aim with his harpoon,
Giulia **crashed her bike** into him!

Seeing their injured friend, Luca and Alberto
came to a **screeching halt**. They climbed off
their bike and rushed to Giulia's side.

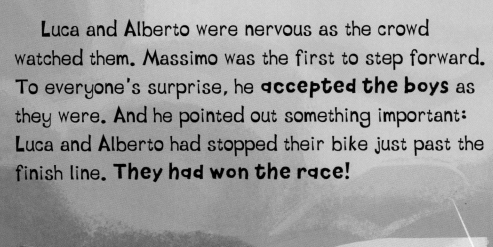

Luca and Alberto were nervous as the crowd watched them. Massimo was the first to step forward. To everyone's surprise, he **accepted the boys** as they were. And he pointed out something important: Luca and Alberto had stopped their bike just past the finish line. **They had won the race!**

Later that evening, Luca and Alberto finally **bought their very own Vespa,** and the group gathered in Massimo's backyard to share a meal. Luca's family was **welcomed with open arms.**

It was soon time for Giulia to go away to school.
But she wasn't the only one. As a surprise, Alberto had
talked to Luca's parents, sold the Vespa, and bought a
train ticket. Luca would be going to school!

Luca wanted his friend to come with him, but Alberto planned to stay in Portorosso with Massimo. Even if they were apart, they knew their **summer memories**—and their **friendship**— would last forever.

Disney · PIXAR
Story Collection 2

Activity Book

Book Quiz

Book Quiz

Disney·Pixar Story Collection 2

Book Quiz

CONTENTS

★북 퀴즈
스토리를 읽고 나서 얼마나 정확히 이해했는지 북 퀴즈를 통해 이해도를 테스트합니다.
스토리의 중심 주제와 세부사항에 관한 문제로,
맞힌 개수에 따라 자신의 독해력을 확인할 수 있어요.

★학습 액티비티
어휘력과 독해력을 길러주는 다양한 문제 액티비티가 수록되었습니다.
또한 이야기 전반을 다시 이해하며 글의 구조를 정리하는 연습을 합니다.

BOOK QUIZ

Frozen

Name: _____ **Date:** _____ / _____ / _____

1. Who had magical powers to create things with snow and ice?

   ① Anna
   ② Elsa
   ③ Olaf
   ④ Kristoff

2. Who did the king and queen rush both girls to see in the mountains?

   ① the mystical trolls
   ② the powerful magicians
   ③ the haunted witches
   ④ the sea monsters

3. What did Elsa's parents give her to help her control her power?

   ① ribbons
   ② jewels
   ③ gloves
   ④ hats

4. Why did Elsa stay away from Anna?

   ① Elsa thought Anna was boring.
   ② Elsa didn't like Anna.
   ③ Elsa didn't want to hurt Anna.
   ④ Elsa liked being alone.

5. Who was excited to meet new people?

   ① Anna   ② Elsa
   ③ Hans   ④ Olaf

6. How did Elsa react when Anna wanted to marry Hans?

   ① She forbade it.
   ② She accepted it.
   ③ She supported it.
   ④ She didn't care at all.

7. Ice and _____ blasted from Elsa's hand.

   ① fire   ② wind
   ③ stones   ④ snow

3

8. Why did Elsa flee?

① She feared she might hurt someone.
② She needed to rest.
③ She wanted more powers.
④ She wanted to look for Kristoff.

9. Anna hired Kristoff to be her _____.

① guide   ② husband
③ servant   ④ chef

10. What did Anna create that made Anna, Kristoff, and Olaf run?

① a giant bear
② a giant snowman
③ a giant tiger
④ a giant palace

11. What color did Anna's hair begin to turn?

① blue   ② green
③ pink   ④ white

12. Who did Anna need for a true love's kiss?

① Elsa   ② her mother
③ Hans   ④ Olaf

13. What was Hans' plan all along?

① to take over the kingdom
② to kill Anna
③ to marry Elsa
④ to steal Elsa's power

14. When the ice melted, Anna realized she was in love with _____.

① Kristoff
② Olaf
③ the guard
④ the king

15. What was the key to controlling Elsa's powers?

① joy
② sadness
③ love
④ music

Score: _____ / 15

• Score 11~15: 이야기를 읽고 세부 내용을 잘 파악하고 있어요.

• Score 6~10: 이야기의 전체적인 흐름을 대체로 잘 파악하고 있어요.

• Score 0~5: 단어 학습을 한 후, 이야기를 다시 한번 읽어 보세요.

BOOK QUIZ

Finding Nemo

Name: _____   **Date:** _____ / _____ / _____

1. Where did Nemo and his father Marlin live?

   ① underwater
   ② above the sea
   ③ in a house
   ④ in the city

2. What kind of fish were Nemo and Marlin?

   ① anglerfish   ② clownfish
   ③ moonfish   ④ janitor fish

3. How did Nemo feel on his first day of school?

   ① He was scared.
   ② He was hungry.
   ③ He was tired.
   ④ He was excited.

4. What did Nemo touch when he swam up to the surface?

   ① a shark   ② a boat
   ③ a human   ④ a dog

5. Looking for help, Marlin swam into all sorts of _____.

   ① fish   ② starfish
   ③ sharks   ④ problems

6. What is the name of the silly fish that helped Marlin?

   ① Flounder   ② Dory
   ③ Jake   ④ Erin

7. Why did Dory think the shark was nice?

   ① The shark gave them a ride.
   ② The shark read them Nemo's address.
   ③ The shark invited them to a party.
   ④ The shark grabbed Nemo.

5

8. What did Marlin and Dory find that belonged to the diver?

   ① a scuba suit   ② a scuba shoe
   ③ a scuba mask   ④ a scuba tank

9. How did the mean anglerfish help Dory?

   ① It helped Dory read an address.
   ② It helped Dory swim faster.
   ③ It helped Dory remember well.
   ④ It helped Dory go above the water.

10. Who gave Marlin and Dory a ride?

   ① some friendly moonfish
   ② some friendly anglerfish
   ③ some friendly turtles
   ④ some friendly sharks

11. Nemo was trapped inside a _____.

   ① fish tank   ② fishing net
   ③ fish bowl   ④ pond

12. Who had the bravest dad in the sea?

   ① the crab
   ② the anglerfish
   ③ the starfish
   ④ the little clownfish

13. Why was it too late when Marlin and Dory arrived?

   ① A little girl had grabbed Nemo.
   ② A little boy had grabbed Nemo.
   ③ A police officer had grabbed Nemo.
   ④ A shark had eaten Nemo.

14. Why was Marlin sad?

   ① He had to separate with Dory.
   ② He didn't like to be alone.
   ③ He thought he would never see Nemo again.
   ④ He lost his way home.

15. When Nemo and Marlin returned home, they were _____.

   ① thieves   ② friends
   ③ heroes   ④ traitors

Score: _____ / 15

• Score 11~15: 이야기를 읽고 세부 내용을 잘 파악하고 있어요.

• Score 6~10: 이야기의 전체적인 흐름을 대체로 잘 파악하고 있어요.

• Score 0~5: 단어 학습을 한 후, 이야기를 다시 한번 읽어 보세요.

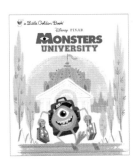

Name: _____ **Date:** _____ / _____ / _____

1. What kind of monster was Mike?

   ① small and green
   ② big and green
   ③ small and black
   ④ big and black

2. Where did Mike learn how to scare?

   ① at Dogs University
   ② at Monsters University
   ③ at Cats University
   ④ at Angels University

3. Mike was a _____ student.

   ① funny   ② boring
   ③ noisy   ④ serious

4. Who did Mike NOT get along with in class?

   ① Art   ② Sulley
   ③ Terri   ④ Don

5. Sulley thought Mike was too little and _____ to be scary.

   ① round   ② lazy
   ③ ugly   ④ cute

6. What grade did Sulley get, while Mike got As?

   ① Cs   ② A⁺s
   ③ Bs   ④ Fs

7. What happened when Mike and Sulley got into a fight during a big test?

   ① They were kicked out of Scaring class.
   ② They both got a perfect score.
   ③ They became great Scarers.
   ④ They gave up their dream.

8. Which team liked Mike?

   ① the Roar Omega Roars
   ② the Oozma Kappas
   ③ the Scare Crew
   ④ the Freaky Scream

9. How many members did the team need to be in the games?

　① eight 　　② seven
　③ six 　　　④ five

10. Where was the first event of the Scare Games held?

　① in the school's sewer
　② in the janitor's closet
　③ in the classroom
　④ in the bathroom

11. Who did Don, Terri, Terry, and Art distract in the second event?

　① the principal
　② the teacher
　③ the policeman
　④ the librarian

12. Where did Mike take the Oozma Kappas on a field trip?

　① to Monsters, Inc
　② to Scary Town
　③ to Sulley's house
　④ to the library

13. What did Sulley pretend to be in the Hide-and-Sneak event?

　① a cat 　　② a dog
　③ a chair 　④ a rug

14. How many teams were left in the last event?

　① two 　　② three
　③ four 　　④ five

15. Why did Sulley worry about Mike?

　① Humans were friendly.
　② Humans were dangerous.
　③ Humans were scary.
　④ Humans were kind.

Score: _____ / 15

- Score 11~15: 이야기를 읽고 세부 내용을 잘 파악하고 있어요.

- Score 6~10: 이야기의 전체적인 흐름을 대체로 잘 파악하고 있어요.

- Score 0~5: 단어 학습을 한 후, 이야기를 다시 한번 읽어 보세요.

Name: _____ **Date:** _____ / _____ / _____

1. What did the Madrigal family call their home?

   ① Visita   ② Casita
   ③ Lavita   ④ Navida

2. Who could heal people with food?

   ① Luisa   ② Isabela
   ③ Abuela   ④ Julieta

3. Isabela could make _____ grow.

   ① flowers   ② trees
   ③ buildings   ④ animals

4. What could Antonio communicate with?

   ① plants   ② animals
   ③ insects   ④ rocks

5. Why did nobody talk about Bruno?

   ① He had been gone for many years.
   ② He was sick.
   ③ He was very mean.
   ④ He didn't have any friends.

6. What happened when Mirabel touched the knob of her glowing door?

   ① She found out her gift.
   ② Casita started to crack.
   ③ The magic went away.
   ④ The candle went out.

7. Who was the only Madrigal without a gift?

   ① Isabela
   ② Mirabel
   ③ Luisa
   ④ Antonio

8. When Mirabel was fifteen, Casita started to crack and _____.

① grow
② shake
③ fall
④ become smaller

9. Who told Mirabel about why Bruno had left Encanto?

① Luisa
② Julieta
③ Isabela
④ Abuela Alma

10. Mirabel was determined to find Bruno's vision _____.

① cave
② ocean
③ door
④ key

11. _____ was in the middle of Bruno's vision puzzle.

① Abuela Alma
② Julieta
③ Mirabel
④ Antonio

12. Where had Bruno been living the whole time?

① in the mountains
② in the walls
③ in the ocean
④ in the sky

13. What did Mirabel and Bruno see in the future?

① a doomed casita
② a happy family
③ a big kingdom
④ a magical horse

14. Bruno told Mirabel to _____ Isabela to see the way.

① hit
② scratch
③ embrace
④ kiss

15. What happened when the candle went out?

① Bruno got hurt.
② The house stopped shaking.
③ Mirabel was powerful.
④ The magic of Casita was gone.

Score: _____ / 15

• Score 11~15: 이야기를 읽고 세부 내용을 잘 파악하고 있어요.

• Score 6~10: 이야기의 전체적인 흐름을 대체로 잘 파악하고 있어요.

• Score 0~5: 단어 학습을 한 후, 이야기를 다시 한번 읽어 보세요.

BOOK QUIZ

Luca

Name: _____   **Date:** _____ / _____ / _____

1. What was Luca the sea monster like?

   ① mean   ② rude
   ③ naughty   ④ friendly

2. Why was Luca forbidden to go on land?

   ① Humans were dangerous.
   ② Luca couldn't swim.
   ③ His parents were gone.
   ④ Humans were kind.

3. What did Alberto accidentally take from Luca?

   ① his gold cup
   ② his shepherding crook
   ③ his diamond stick
   ④ his seashell

4. When Luca and Alberto reached land, they transformed into _____.

   ① dogs   ② cats
   ③ horses   ④ humans

5. Where did Alberto take Luca after they had turned into humans?

   ① to his house
   ② to his grandma's house
   ③ to his hideout
   ④ to his store

6. What did the boys realize they could build?

   ① their own Vespa
   ② their own house
   ③ their own boat
   ④ their own truck

7. Luca's parents decided to make Luca live with his _____.

   ① aunt
   ② uncle
   ③ grandmother
   ④ grandfather

8. Who did Luca and Alberto meet at the seaside town of Portorosso?

① Helen   ② Giulia
③ Margaret   ④ Catherine

9. What was Massimo's job?

① a fisherman   ② a farmer
③ a doctor   ④ a policeman

10. Why did Machiavelli keep a close eye on the boys?

① He was curious about them.
② He liked them.
③ He smelled something fishy.
④ He wanted to join them.

11. Who was the five-time race champion?

① Machiavelli   ② Massimo
③ Ercole   ④ Ernist

12. What did Luca practice for the race?

① swimming
② eating pasta
③ riding a bike
④ dancing

13. What did Ercole throw at Alberto?

① his stone
② his bat
③ his harpoon
④ his stick

14. In the race, Luca wore a _____ to avoid transforming in the water.

① diving suit
② necktie
③ swimsuit
④ belt

15. Who won the Portorosso Race?

① Luca's team
② Ercole's team
③ Maxine's team
④ Jose's team

Score: _____ / 15

- Score 11~15: 이야기를 읽고 세부 내용을 잘 파악하고 있어요.

- Score 6~10: 이야기의 전체적인 흐름을 대체로 잘 파악하고 있어요.

- Score 0~5: 단어 학습을 한 후, 이야기를 다시 한번 읽어 보세요.

Activities

A 다음 단어의 알맞은 우리말 뜻에 동그라미 하세요.

1 change (흔들리다 / 바꾸다)

2 forbid (금지하다 / 끝마치다)

3 fault (축복 / 잘못)

4 save (구하다 / 무너지다)

5 refuse (거절하다 / 인정하다)

6 control (잊어버리다 / 통제하다)

7 memory (기억 / 기적)

8 lonely (행복한 / 외로운)

B 빈칸에 알맞은 단어를 써 넣어 퍼즐을 완성하세요.

Across	① 마법의	② 용기	③ 달아나다
Down	④ 녹다	⑤ 왕국	⑥ 얼어붙은

C 다음 단어를 사용하여 문장을 완성하세요.

| spell | expose | hurt | danger | create | crown |

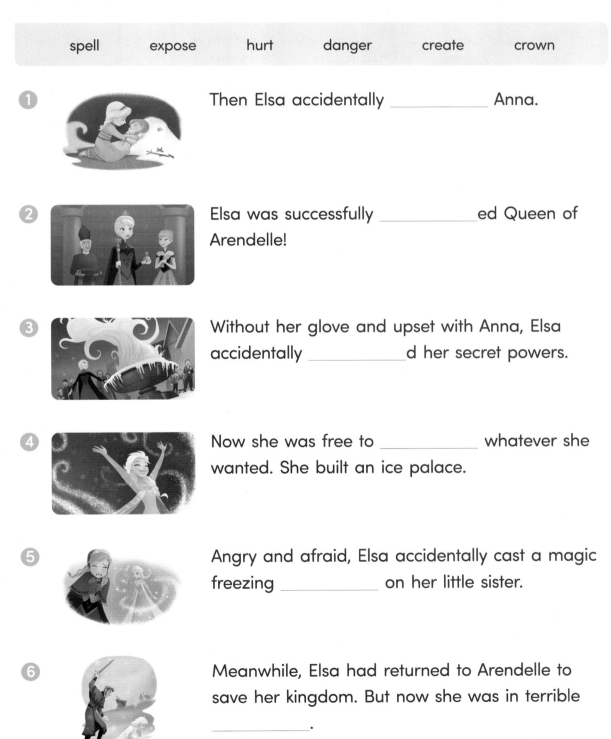

1 Then Elsa accidentally _____ Anna.

2 Elsa was successfully _____ed Queen of Arendelle!

3 Without her glove and upset with Anna, Elsa accidentally _____d her secret powers.

4 Now she was free to _____ whatever she wanted. She built an ice palace.

5 Angry and afraid, Elsa accidentally cast a magic freezing _____ on her little sister.

6 Meanwhile, Elsa had returned to Arendelle to save her kingdom. But now she was in terrible _____.

STORY Check

A 다음 일들의 원인을 찾아 맞게 연결해 보세요.

1 Elsa could create things out of snow and ice!

2 Ice and snow blasted from her hand, covering the kingdom.

3 Anna and Kristoff ran. Olaf ran, too!

ⓐ Without her glove and upset with Anna, Elsa exposed her secret powers.

ⓑ Elsa accidentally cast a magic freezing spell on her little sister and then created a giant snowman.

ⓒ Elsa had magical powers.

B 이야기의 순서에 맞게 알맞은 기호를 찾아 쓰세요.

ⓐ Fearing she might hurt someone and ruin her kingdom, Elsa fled.

ⓑ Elsa was free to create whatever she wanted. She built an ice palace.

ⓒ Anna hired a mountain man named Kristoff to be her guide.

ⓓ To help her control it, Elsa's parents gave her gloves.

C 다음 글에 알맞은 그림을 찾아 연결하세요.

1
The trolls cautioned that others would fear Elsa's power.

2
Elsa gathered all her courage to take off her gloves and was successfully crowned Queen of Arendelle!

3
Frustrated, Anna tried to stop her sister and accidentally pulled off one glove.

4
Anna and Kristoff found a snowman named Olaf. He was alive!

5
Meanwhile, Elsa had returned to Arendelle to save her kingdom. But she was in terrible danger.

6
Anna realized she was in love with Kristoff. As for Elsa, she became queen again.

SENTENCE Check

A 알맞은 단어에 동그라미 하여 문장을 완성하세요.

1. The trolls cured Anna by changing her memories of Elsa's [magic / name] .

2. Years later, the king and queen were [found / lost] at sea.

3. Anna, on the other hand, was excited to [meet / help] new people.

4. Anna rushed off to find her [parents / sister] .

5. She hired a mountain man named Kristoff to be her [guide / friend] .

6. Anna begged Elsa to go home to [thaw / see] her frozen kingdom.

7. Kristoff led her to the trolls for [exercise / help] .

8. Hans' plan all along had been to [look / take] over the kingdom.

9. It was an act of true love — true [love / test] between two sisters.

10. Love was the key to controlling her [fear / powers] .

18

B 다음 단어들을 이용해 우리말 뜻에 맞는 문장을 완성하세요.

1

| a snowman | she | Olaf | made | named | . |

그녀는 올라프라는 이름의 눈사람을 만들었어요.

→ _____

2

| gloves | Elsa's | gave | parents | her | . |

엘사의 부모님은 그녀에게 장갑을 주었어요.

→ _____

3

| Anna | to stop | her sister | tried | . |

안나는 그녀의 언니를 막으려고 했어요.

→ _____

4

| to Elsa | the way | Olaf | led | . |

올라프는 엘사에게로 가는 길을 안내했어요.

→ _____

5

| to turn | white | began | Anna's hair | . |

안나의 머리카락이 하얗게 변하기 시작했어요.

→ _____

6

| control | Elsa feared | her powers | she couldn't | . |

엘사는 자신의 힘을 통제할 수 없어서 두려웠어요.

→ _____

STORY MAP

문장의 빈칸을 채워 이야기의 구조를 한눈에 정리해 보세요.

| saved | advised | kingdom | snow | spell | gloves |

Characters

The main characters are Anna, Elsa, and Kristoff.

Setting

This story started in the ① _____ of Arendelle.

Problem

Elsa had magical powers to create things out of ② _____ and ice. Elsa's parents gave her gloves to help her control the power.

It was time for Elsa to take over as Queen. Anna accidentally pulled off one of Elsa's ③ _____. Elsa exposed her secret powers. Fearing she might hurt someone and ruin her kingdom, Elsa fled.

Ending

Anna begged Elsa to go home to thaw her frozen kingdom. But Elsa accidentally cast a magic freezing ④ _____ on her little sister.

Anna's hair began to turn white. The trolls ⑤ _____ that only an act of true love could thaw a frozen heart. Kristoff and Anna headed back to Arendelle.

Meanwhile, Elsa had returned to Arendelle to save her kingdom. But she was in terrible danger. In the end, Anna ⑥ _____ Elsa. It was an act of true love between two sisters.

Activities

WORD Check

A 다음 단어의 알맞은 우리말 뜻에 동그라미 하세요.

1. scared (희귀한 / 무서워하는)
2. spread (모으다 / 퍼지다)
3. harbor (학교 / 항구)
4. return (돌아오다 / 탈출하다)
5. disappear (만들다 / 사라지다)
6. surface (책상 / 수면)
7. shape (배 / 모양)
8. address (기억 / 주소)

B 빈칸에 알맞은 단어를 써 넣어 퍼즐을 완성하세요.

Across	① 삼키다	② 탈출하다	③ 바다
Down	④ 매우 기쁘게 하다	⑤ 살금살금 가다	⑥ ~에 속하다

① s
④ o
⑥ b
② e
⑤ s
③ o
a

22

다음 단어를 사용하여 문장을 완성하세요.

| remember | swam | repeat | ride | fish tank | spotted |

1. Dori was so excited that she _____ed the address over and over.

2. Today was Nemo's first day of school! On the way there he saw a _____ fish.

3. Nemo wanted to escape from the _____ where he was trapped.

4. Looking for help, Marlin _____ into all sorts of fish.

5. Dori was a little bit silly, and she couldn't _____ very much, but she was happy to help Marlin!

6. Some friendly turtles gave Marlin and Dory a _____.

STORY Check

A 동물들이 어떻게 Marlin과 Dory를 도와줬는지 정리해 보세요.

How Marlin and Dory Got Help

	The light was attached to a mean ① _____! It helped Dory ② _____ an address written on the mask.
	Marlin and Dori met some ③ _____. They ④ _____ toward 42 Wallaby Way, Sydney.
	Some friendly ⑤ _____ gave Marlin and Dory a ride.
	A ⑥ _____ swallowed Marlin and Dory! He took them all the way to ⑦ _____!
	A ⑧ _____ helped Marlin and Dory go straight to 42 Wallaby Way, Sydney.

pelican	turtles	whale	anglerfish
moonfish	pointed	read	Sydney Harbor

B 다음 글에 알맞은 그림을 찾아 연결하세요.

1 Marlin was scared of the big fish, so he always kept Nemo close to him.

2 Marlin tried to save his son, but the boat sped away so fast it soon disappeared.

3 One friendly fish named Dory swam down to see if Marlin was okay.

4 Marlin told the story of his search for Nemo, and the news spread across the ocean!

5 Marlin was sad. He thought he would never see his son again.

6 When they finally returned home, both Nemo and Marlin were heroes.

A 알맞은 단어에 동그라미 하여 문장을 완성하세요.

1. Because they were clownfish, they were [small / slow] .

2. Nemo and his friends sneaked away and swam to the really [deep / dirty] water.

3. The only thing on Marlin's mind now was [finding / teaching] Nemo.

4. Dory thought it was very nice of the [shell / shark] to invite them to a party.

5. The light was attached to a [friendly / mean] anglerfish!

6. Some friendly [whales / turtles] gave Marlin and Dory a ride.

7. The little clownfish was bursting with [energy / pride] . He had the bravest dad in the sea!

8. The [whale / boat] took them as close as he could get to 42 Wallaby Way, Sydney.

9. Marlin was sad. He thought he would never see his son [again / before] .

10. When they finally returned home, both Nemo and Marlin were [friends / heroes] .

B 다음 단어들을 이용해 우리말 뜻에 맞는 문장을 완성하세요.

1

| lived | and | Nemo | underwater | his father Marlin | . |

니모와 니모의 아빠 멀린은 물 밑에서 살았어요.

→ _____

2

| him | Nemo | and | scolded | Marlin | chased after | . |

멀린은 니모를 쫓아가 야단을 쳤어요.

→ _____

3

| in the boat | was | Nemo | taken away | . |

니모는 배 안으로 없어져버렸어요.

→ _____

4

| Nemo's | excited, | new friends | too | were | . |

니모의 새로운 친구들도 매우 신이 났어요.

→ _____

5

| was scared | Marlin | the big fish | of | . |

멀린은 큰 물고기들이 무서웠어요.

→ _____

6

| Nemo's class | the science teacher | on a field trip | took | . |

과학 선생님이 니모네 반을 현장학습에 데려갔어요.

→ _____

STORY MAP

문장의 빈칸을 채워 이야기의 구조를 한눈에 정리해 보세요.

field trip	helped	escaped	address
grabbed	swam	mask	caught

Problem

When Nemo went on a ① _____,
he swam way up to the surface of the
ocean. Then he got ② _____! He was
taken away in a boat.

Solution

Marlin and Dori ③ _____ to look for Nemo
together.
They found a scuba ④ _____ that belonged
to the diver who had taken Nemo.
They read an ⑤ _____ written on the
mask. It was 42 Wallaby
Way, Sydney.

Many animals helped Marlin and Dory
reach the address.
A pelican named Nigel ⑥ _____ Marlin and
Dory go straight to 42 Wallaby Way, Sydney.

Ending

A little girl had ⑦ _____ Nemo.
Marlin was sad. He thought he would never
see his son again.
But Nemo had ⑧ _____! Dory found him.
They were overjoyed.

28

Disney·PIXAR

MONSTERS UNIVERSITY

Activities

A 다음 단어의 알맞은 우리말 뜻에 동그라미 하세요.

① ceiling　(바닥 / 천장)　　**②** vanish　(나타나다 / 사라지다)

③ prove　(증명하다 / 증가하다)　　**④** cheat　(속이다 / 추가하다)

⑤ fail　(합격하다 / 떨어지다)　　**⑥** thrilled　(아주 신이 난 / 우울한)

⑦ university　(대회 / 대학)　　**⑧** roar　(올라감 / 으르렁거림)

B 빈칸에 알맞은 단어를 써 넣어 퍼즐을 완성하세요.

Across	① 주의를 돌리다	② 무서운	③ 이기다	④ 진지한
Down	⑤ 비명; 비명을 지르다		⑥ 캠퍼스, 교정	

⑥ c

① d　⑤ s

② s

③ b　④ s

C 다음 단어를 사용하여 문장을 완성하세요.

| scare | powerful | eliminate | kick | argue | pretend |

① Sulley and Mike were _____ed out of Scaring class.

② Mike and Sulley came up with a plan that would _____ the pants off the camp rangers.

③ While Mike and Sulley _____d about the best way to win, the other Oozma Kappas worked together.

④ One by one, the other teams were getting _____d from the Scare Games.

⑤ In the Hide-and-Sneak event, Sulley _____ed to be a rug.

⑥ But now they were friends. And they made a _____ team.

A Mike와 Sulley의 공통점과 차이점을 구별해서 써보세요.

test	green	blue	played	worked	parties

Mike

Sulley

Mike was ① _____.

Mike was round.

Mike ② _____ hard.

Mike studied.

Mike got As.

Both monsters failed a big
③ _____.

They were kicked out of Scaring class.

Sulley was ④ _____.

Sulley was big.

Sulley ⑤ _____.

Sulley went to ⑥ _____.

Sulley got Cs.

B 이야기와 일치하는 문장에는 T, 일치하지 않는 문장에는 F에 동그라미 하세요.

① Sulley and Mike were kicked out of Scaring class.   T   F

② In the end, Mike gave up his dream.   T   F

③ Mike had to join one of the school's teams to compete in the Scare Games.   T   F

④ Sulley didn't want to get back into Scaring class.   T   F

C 다음 글에 알맞은 그림을 찾아 연결하세요.

1 During a big test, Mike and Sulley got into a fight.

2 Only Sulley looked like a real Scarer.

3 Don, Terri, Terry, and Art distracted the librarian while Squishy grabbed the flag!

4 The Oozma Kappas were coming together as a team. And their hard work paid off.

5 Mike and Sulley practiced and practiced. Still, Sulley was worried.

6 The greatest Scarers in the world worked there—and they looked nothing alike!

A 알맞은 단어에 동그라미 하여 문장을 완성하세요.

① But Mike had plans, ⌈ big / fun ⌉ plans.

② Mike couldn't wait to prove Sulley ⌈ wrong / strong ⌉ !

③ During a big test, Mike and Sulley got into a ⌈ sewer / fight ⌉ .

④ Mike wasn't ready to give up his ⌈ dream / job ⌉ .

⑤ The Oozma Kappas were the least ⌈ ugly / scary ⌉ monsters on campus.

⑥ The Oozma Kappas were coming together as a ⌈ band / team ⌉ .

⑦ Don stuck himself flat against the ⌈ ceiling / wall ⌉ .

⑧ Mike was ⌈ thrilled / worried ⌉ to get a huge scream in the event.

⑨ Mike decided to ⌈ tell / show ⌉ everyone how scary he was.

⑩ But they both got ⌈ hurt / trapped ⌉ in the human world.

B 다음 단어들을 이용해 우리말 뜻에 맞는 문장을 완성하세요.

1

| was | Mike | student | serious | a | . |

마이크는 진지한 학생이었어요.

→ _____

2

| except Sulley | liked everything | he | about school | . |

그는 설리를 제외하고 학교에 관한 모든 것이 좋았어요.

→ _____

3

| lazy | Mike thought | was | Sulley | . |

마이크는 설리가 게으르다고 생각했어요.

→ _____

4

| both | to win | Sulley and Mike | wanted | . |

설리와 마이크는 둘 다 이기고 싶어했어요.

→ _____

5

| they | got trapped | both | in the human world | . |

그들은 둘 다 인간 세계에 갇히고 말았어요.

→ _____

6

| found out | Sulley | that | had cheated | he | ! |

그는 설리가 속였다는 것을 알게 됐어요!

→ _____

문장의 빈칸을 채워 이야기의 구조를 한눈에 정리해 보세요.

| scream | failed | mad | human | poster | dangerous |

Problem

During a big test, Mike and Sulley got into a fight. Both monsters ① _____ !
They were kicked out of Scaring class.

Sulley changed the settings in the scare room to make it easier for Mike.
Mike was ③ _____ because Sulley didn't believe in him.

Sulley was worried about Mike. Humans were ⑤ _____ !
So Sulley followed Mike. But they both got trapped in the human world.

Solution

Mike saw a ② _____ for the Scare Games. Winning the Scare Games would prove he was scary. Then the university would have to let him back into Scaring class!

Mike decided to show everyone how scary he was. Mike snuck through a forbidden door and into the ④ _____ world. Mike tried out his best scare—"Roar!"

Only an enormous ⑥ _____ could open the door back to Monsters University. Mike and Sulley came up with a plan that would scare the camp rangers.

Activities

A 다음 단어의 알맞은 우리말 뜻에 동그라미 하세요.

1 shake   (흔들리다 / 빼내다)

2 revelation   (성공 / 폭로)

3 glow   (자라다 / 빛나다)

4 pray   (기도하다 / 축하하다)

5 crumble   (잡아당기다 / 무너지다)

6 proudly   (자랑스럽게 / 중요한)

7 passageway   (통로 / 감각)

8 gift   (영혼 / 재능)

B 빈칸에 알맞은 단어를 써 넣어 퍼즐을 완성하세요.

Across	① 회복시키다	② 혼돈, 혼란	③ 치유하다
Down	④ 다시 세우다	⑤ 가치가 있는	⑥ 환상, 예지력

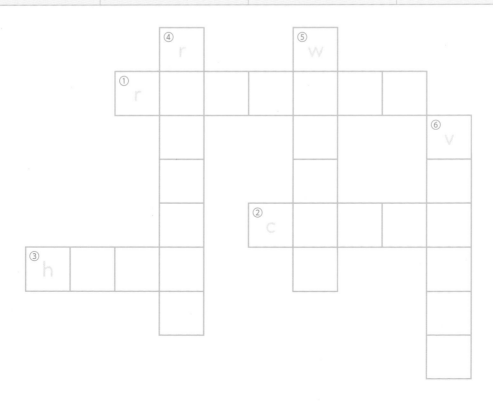

C 다음 단어를 사용하여 문장을 완성하세요.

destroyed	miracle	embrace
crack	communicate	future

1
Bruno could see the _____. But nobody talked about Bruno.

2
One day, when Mirabel was fifteen, Casita started to _____.

3
The puzzle revealed a _____ Casita, and in the middle was Mirabel!

4
"_____ her and you will see the way," said Bruno.

5
Antonio could _____ with animals.

6
Abuela told Mirabel about that night long ago, how she had prayed for a _____.

A 등장인물에 해당하는 그림과 설명을 연결하세요.

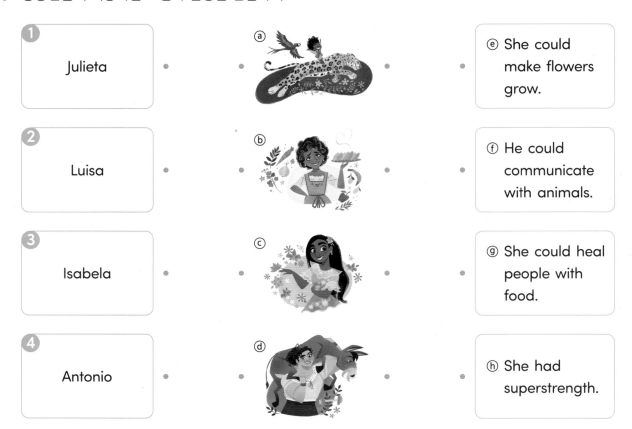

① Julieta

② Luisa

③ Isabela

④ Antonio

ⓐ

ⓑ

ⓒ

ⓓ

ⓔ She could make flowers grow.

ⓕ He could communicate with animals.

ⓖ She could heal people with food.

ⓗ She had superstrength.

B 이야기와 일치하는 문장에는 T, 일치하지 않는 문장에는 F에 동그라미 하세요.

① Abuela Alma had been gone for many years.　　T　F

② Mirabel was the only Madrigal without a gift.　　T　F

③ When Mirabel was fifteen, Casita started to crack.　　T　F

④ Mirabel gave up looking for Bruno's vision cave.　　T　F

C 다음 글에 알맞은 그림을 찾아 연결하세요.

1 Mirabel was the only Madrigal without a gift. This made her feel like she wasn't special enough or worthy enough.

2 Mirabel had an idea. If she found the reason for the cracks, she could fix them and prove she was special!

3 The candle went out. All the magic of Casita was gone!

4 Abuela felt that if the family was strong enough and worked hard enough, she could protect them.

5 Nobody could believe what they saw: Abuela, proudly walking alongside Mirabel and Bruno!

6 Casita came back to life, and the Encanto's magic was restored.

A 알맞은 단어에 동그라미 하여 문장을 완성하세요.

① In a small village deep in the wilderness, an ever-glowing [candle / moon] shone brightly.

② Mirabel and Abuela Alma were so excited to find out what her [gift / name] was!

③ There, she found glowing pieces of Bruno's broken [vision / house].

④ Mirabel asked Bruno to look into the [cave / future].

⑤ Isabela told her that she always felt she could never be [perfect / pretty] enough for Abuela.

⑥ The family members raced to save the candle, but their powers were [facing / fading].

⑦ Losing Abuelo broke something inside Abuela that no magic flame could ever [repair / reveal].

⑧ "We were given a [miracle / problem] because of you," Mirabel told Abuela.

⑨ They all worked together to [rebuild / paint] Casita.

⑩ And at last, Mirabel felt her own [goal / worth] and her family's love.

B 다음 단어들을 이용해 우리말 뜻에 맞는 문장을 완성하세요.

1 | powerful | was | its magic | so | . |

그것의 마법은 매우 강력했어요.

→ _____

2 | Julieta | could heal | with food | people | . |

줄리에타는 음식으로 사람들을 치유할 수 있었어요.

→ _____

3 | in danger | the house | is | . |

집이 위험했어요.

→ _____

4 | light | glowed | the | candle's | brighter | . |

촛불의 불빛이 더욱 밝게 빛났어요.

→ _____

5 | Encanto | entire | shook | the | . |

엔칸토 전체가 흔들렸어요.

→ _____

6 | I feel like | important | I missed | something | . |

뭔가 중요한 걸 놓친 것 같은 기분이 들어요.

→ _____

STORY MAP

문장의 빈칸을 채워 이야기의 구조를 한눈에 정리해 보세요.

family	Encanto	gift	husband	fear	crack

Characters

The main characters are Mirabel, Abuela Alma, and Bruno.

Setting

This story took place in ① _____.

Problem

Mirabel was the only Madrigal without a ② _____.

This made her feel like she wasn't special enough or worthy enough.

Casita started to ③ _____. Then it had crumbled into a pile of rubble and dust. The entire Encanto shook.

Solution

At a nearby riverbank, Abuela found Mirabel. Abuela Alma said it was where she had lost her ④ _____, Abuelo Pedro.

Abuela Alma realized her broken heart had made her live in ⑤ _____.

Mirabel, Abuela Alma, and Bruno headed home. Everyone realized what made them special was their ⑥ _____ bond.

Activities

WORD Check

A 다음 단어의 알맞은 우리말 뜻에 동그라미 하세요.

1 unsure (의심스러워하는 / 가득한)

2 shocked (충격을 받은 / 거대한)

3 complete (사라지다 / 완료하다)

4 rescue (구조하다 / 위로하다)

5 friendship (우정 / 축복)

6 accept (기대하다 / 받아들이다)

7 practice (축하하다 / 연습하다)

8 treasure (보물 / 악기)

B 빈칸에 알맞은 단어를 써 넣어 퍼즐을 완성하세요.

Across	① 금지하다	② 비밀 은신처	③ 위험
Down	④ 충돌하다	⑤ 수상한	⑥ 놀란

C 다음 단어를 사용하여 문장을 완성하세요.

| hide | transform | zoom | soar | bought | taunt |

1 When they reached land, Luca and Alberto _____ed into humans!

2 They even rode one together and _____ed through the air!

3 The bully _____ed the three friends and vowed to defeat them.

4 Luca decided to race alone to protect Giulia. It was risky to _____ his sea monster identity.

5 During the bike race, Luca _____ed ahead, passing racers left and right.

6 Luca and Alberto finally _____ their very own Vespa.

STORY Check

A Luca가 어떻게 문제를 해결했는지 맞게 연결해 보세요.

Problem

Solution

① Luca's parents decided Luca would be safer living deep in the ocean with his uncle.

ⓐ

ⓓ Before they could send him away, Luca left to find Alberto.

② Ercole taunted the three friends and vowed to defeat them.

ⓑ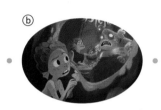

ⓔ Luca wouldn't give up. He promised to get Alberto and Giulia a Vespa.

③ Alberto was angry at Luca and didn't want to race anymore.

ⓒ

ⓕ More determined than ever, the team began training for the three events of the Portorosso Cup.

B 아래 등장인물에 해당하는 문장을 찾아 맞게 기호를 써보세요.

ⓐ Though I dreamed about life above the surface, I was forbidden to go on land.

ⓑ I was unsure about the boys at first, but I soon realized that we would be perfect teammates for a local race called the Portorosso Cup.

ⓒ I took Luca to my hideout. It was full of neat human things.

❶  ☐

❷  ☐

❸  ☐

C 다음 글에 알맞은 그림을 찾아 연결하세요.

1 Luca was a friendly sea monster. He spent his days herding a flock of goatfish.

2 As Alberto collected some new treasures, he accidentally took Luca's shepherding crook.

3 Massimo's cat, Machiavelli, kept a close eye on the boys. He smelled something fishy!

4 Ercole ran up and threw his harpoon. Alberto escaped just in time.

5 Giulia soon figured out that Luca was a sea monster, too.

6 Alberto's hideout was full of neat human things, including a poster of a shiny Vespa.

 **SENTENCE Check**

A 알맞은 단어에 동그라미 하여 문장을 완성하세요.

1. Luca's parents warned him that [goatfish / humans] were dangerous.

2. Luca [chased / rode] him all the way to the surface!

3. They even rode Vespas together and soared through the [air / park].

4. Luca's parents decided Luca would be safer living [deep / alone] in the ocean with his uncle.

5. With the [pocket / prize] money, they could buy a real Vespa.

6. Luca and Alberto knew that winning wasn't going to be [easy / difficult].

7. Giulia soon figured out that Luca was a [dangerous / sea] monster, too.

8. During the [car / bike] race, Luca zoomed ahead, passing racers left and right.

9. Seeing their injured friend, Luca and Alberto came to a screeching [halt / hand].

10. Luca's family was welcomed with open [arms / shoulders].

50

B 다음 단어들을 이용해 우리말 뜻에 맞는 문장을 완성하세요.

1

| on land | to go | was forbidden | Luca | . |

루카는 육지에 가는 것이 금지되었어요.

→ _____

2

| around Luca | was strange | everything | but amazing | . |

루카 주변의 모든 것들이 신기하면서도 놀라웠어요.

→ _____

3

| something | smelled | fishy | He | . |

그는 뭔가 수상쩍은 냄새를 맡았어요.

→ _____

4

| they | over time, | good friends | became | . |

시간이 흐르면서, 그들은 좋은 친구가 되었어요.

→ _____

5

| Alberto | in a net | a crowd | trapped | . |

사람들이 알베르토를 그물에 가두었어요.

→ _____

6

| to avoid | he wore | in the water | a diving suit | transforming | . |

그는 물속에서 변신하는 것을 피하기 위해 잠수복을 입었어요.

→ _____

문장의 빈칸을 채워 이야기 구조를 한눈에 정리해 보세요.

school	taunted	bike	race	monster

Beginning

Luca, Alberto, and Giulia decided to enter the Portorosso Cup.
But Ercole ① _____ the three friends and vowed to defeat them.

Problem

Alberto didn't want to race in the Portorosso Cup because he didn't want Luca to go to ② _____ with Giulia.

During the ③ _____ race, it began to rain. Alberto came to help Luca. But the rain transformed Alberto into a sea monster.
A crowd trapped Alberto in a net.

Luca rescued his friend. Giulia crashed her bike into Ercole when he took aim at Luca and Alberto with his harpoon. But everyone knew Luca was a sea ④ _____, too.

Ending

Giulia's father accepted Luca and Alberto as they were. Finally, Luca and Alberto won the ⑤ _____!

The Answers

BOOK QUIZ

Frozen Book Quiz   p.3

1. ②	2. ①	3. ③	4. ③	5. ①	6. ①
7. ④	8. ①	9. ①	10. ②	11. ④	12. ③
13. ①	14. ①	15. ③			

Finding Nemo Book Quiz   p.5

1. ①	2. ②	3. ④	4. ②	5. ①	6. ②
7. ③	8. ③	9. ①	10. ③	11. ①	12. ④
13. ①	14. ③	15. ③			

Monsters University Book Quiz   p.7

1. ①	2. ②	3. ④	4. ②	5. ④	6. ①
7. ①	8. ②	9. ③	10. ①	11. ④	12. ①
13. ④	14. ①	15. ②			

Encanto Book Quiz   p.9

1. ②	2. ④	3. ①	4. ②	5. ①	6. ③
7. ②	8. ②	9. ①	10. ①	11. ③	12. ②
13. ①	14. ③	15. ④			

Luca Book Quiz   p.11

1. ④	2. ①	3. ②	4. ④	5. ③	6. ①
7. ②	8. ②	9. ①	10. ③	11. ③	12. ③
13. ③	14. ①	15. ①			

FROZEN Activities

WORD Check p.14

A ① 바꾸다 ② 금지하다
③ 잘못 ④ 구하다
⑤ 거절하다 ⑥ 통제하다
⑦ 기억 ⑧ 외로운

B

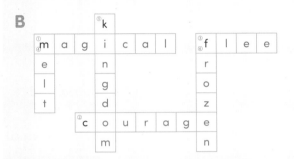

C ① hurt ② crown
③ expose ④ create
⑤ spell ⑥ danger

STORY Check p.16

A ① ⓒ ② ⓐ
③ ⓑ

B ⓓ → ⓐ → ⓒ → ⓑ

C ① ⓑ ② ⓐ
③ ⓕ ④ ⓔ
⑤ ⓒ ⑥ ⓓ

SENTENCE Check p.18

A ① magic ② lost
③ meet ④ sister
⑤ guide ⑥ thaw
⑦ help ⑧ take
⑨ love ⑩ powers

B ① She made a snowman named Olaf.
② Elsa's parents gave her gloves.
③ Anna tried to stop her sister.
④ Olaf led the way to Elsa.
⑤ Anna's hair began to turn white.
⑥ Elsa feared she couldn't control her powers.

STORY MAP p.20

① kingdom
② snow
③ gloves
④ spell
⑤ advised
⑥ saved

FINDING NEMO Activities

WORD Check · · · · · · · · · · · · · · · · · · p.22

A ① 무서워하는 ② 퍼지다
③ 항구 ④ 돌아오다
⑤ 사라지다 ⑥ 수면
⑦ 모양 ⑧ 주소

B

① s	w	a	l	l	④ o	w
					v	
			② e	③ s	c	a	p	e
				n		
				e		
③ o	c	e	a	n		
				y		

⑥ b / e / l / o / n / g

C ① repeat ② spotted
③ fish tank ④ swam
⑤ remember ⑥ ride

SENTENCE Check · · · · · · · · · · · · · · p.26

A ① small ② deep
③ finding ④ shark
⑤ mean ⑥ turtles
⑦ pride ⑧ whale
⑨ again ⑩ heroes

B ① Nemo and his father Marlin lived underwater.
② Marlin chased after Nemo and scolded him.
③ Nemo was taken away in the boat.
④ Nemo's new friends were excited, too.
⑤ Marlin was scared of the big fish.
⑥ The science teacher took Nemo's class on a field trip.

STORY Check · · · · · · · · · · · · · · · · · p.24

A ① anglerfish ② read
③ moonfish ④ pointed
⑤ turtles ⑥ whale
⑦ Sydney Harbor ⑧ pelican

B ① ⓒ ② ⓓ
③ ⓐ ④ ⓑ
⑤ ⓕ ⑥ ⓔ

STORY MAP · · · · · · · · · · · · · · · · · · p.28

① field trip
② caught
③ swam
④ mask
⑤ address
⑥ helped
⑦ grabbed
⑧ escaped

MONSTERS UNIVERSITY Activities

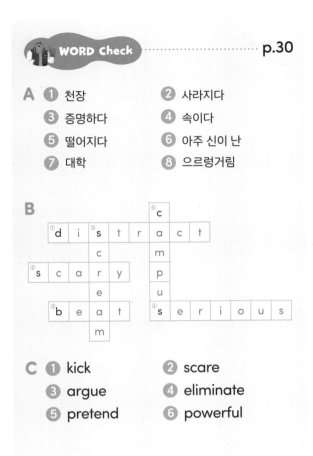

WORD Check p.30

A ① 천장　　② 사라지다
　　③ 증명하다　　④ 속이다
　　⑤ 떨어지다　　⑥ 아주 신이 난
　　⑦ 대학　　⑧ 으르렁거림

B

		c				
d	i	s	t	r	a	c	t

Across/Down crossword:
- d i s t r a c t
- c / m
- s c a r y / m p u
- e
- b e a t / s e r i o u s
- m

C ① kick　　② scare
　　③ argue　　④ eliminate
　　⑤ pretend　　⑥ powerful

SENTENCE Check p.34

A ① big　　② wrong
　　③ fight　　④ dream
　　⑤ scary　　⑥ team
　　⑦ ceiling　　⑧ thrilled
　　⑨ show　　⑩ trapped

B ① Mike was a serious student.
② He liked everything about school except Sulley.
③ Mike thought Sulley was lazy.
④ Both Sulley and Mike wanted to win.
⑤ They both got trapped in the human world.
⑥ He found out that Sulley had cheated!

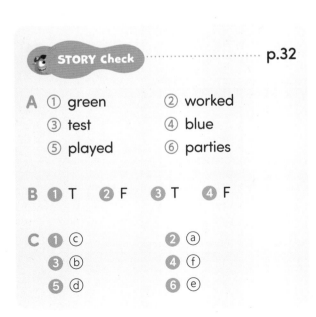

STORY Check p.32

A ① green　　② worked
　　③ test　　④ blue
　　⑤ played　　⑥ parties

B ① T　② F　③ T　④ F

C ① ⓒ　　② ⓐ
　　③ ⓑ　　④ ⓕ
　　⑤ ⓓ　　⑥ ⓔ

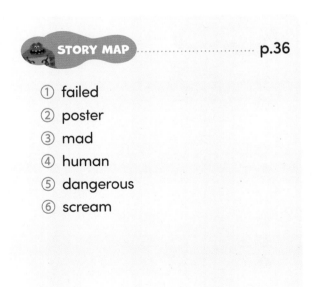

STORY MAP p.36

① failed
② poster
③ mad
④ human
⑤ dangerous
⑥ scream

ENCANTO Activities

WORD Check p.38

A ① 흔들리다   ② 폭로
  ③ 빛나다   ④ 기도하다
  ⑤ 무너지다   ⑥ 자랑스럽게
  ⑦ 통로   ⑧ 재능

B
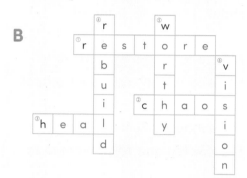

C ① future   ② crack
  ③ destroyed   ④ Embrace
  ⑤ communicate   ⑥ miracle

STORY Check p.40

A ①-ⓑ-ⓖ   ②-ⓓ-ⓗ
  ③-ⓒ-ⓔ   ④-ⓐ-ⓕ

B ① F   ② T
  ③ T   ④ F

C ① ⓑ   ② ⓓ
  ③ ⓐ   ④ ⓒ
  ⑤ ⓔ   ⑥ ⓕ

SENTENCE Check p.42

A ① candle   ② gift
  ③ vision   ④ future
  ⑤ perfect   ⑥ fading
  ⑦ repair   ⑧ miracle
  ⑨ rebuild   ⑩ worth

B ① Its magic was so powerful.
  ② Julieta could heal people with food.
  ③ The house is in danger.
  ④ The candle's light glowed brighter.
  ⑤ The entire Encanto shook.
  ⑥ I feel like I missed something important.

STORY MAP p.44

① Encanto
② gift
③ crack
④ husband
⑤ fear
⑥ family

LUCA Activities

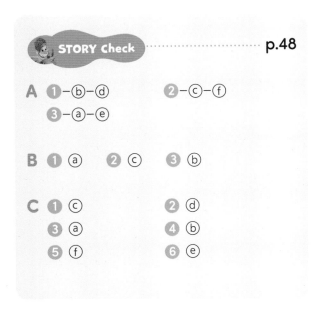

WORD Check ········· p.46

A ① 의심스러워하는 ② 충격을 받은
③ 완료하다 ④ 구조하다
⑤ 우정 ⑥ 받아들이다
⑦ 연습하다 ⑧ 보물

B

Crossword:
d a n g e r
c · f · m
f o r b i d a · a
a · s · z
s · h i d e o u t
h · y · d

C ① transform ② soar
③ taunt ④ hide
⑤ zoom ⑥ bought

STORY Check ········· p.48

A ① -ⓑ-ⓓ ② -ⓒ-ⓕ
③ -ⓐ-ⓔ

B ① ⓐ ② ⓒ ③ ⓑ

C ① ⓒ ② ⓓ
③ ⓐ ④ ⓑ
⑤ ⓕ ⑥ ⓔ

SENTENCE Check ········· p.50

A ① humans ② chased
③ air ④ deep
⑤ prize ⑥ easy
⑦ sea ⑧ bike
⑨ halt ⑩ arms

B ① Luca was forbidden to go on land.
② Everything around Luca was strange but amazing.
③ He smelled something fishy.
④ Over time, they became good friends.
⑤ A crowd trapped Alberto in a net.
⑥ He wore a diving suit to avoid transforming in the water.

STORY MAP ········· p.52

① taunted
② school
③ bike
④ monster
⑤ race

Activity Book

Part 1 북 퀴즈(Book Quiz)

읽은 내용을 얼마나 잘 이해했는지 북 퀴즈를 풀며 나의 리딩 실력을 점검합니다.
틀린 문제는 스토리북의 해당 내용을 다시 찾아 읽어보세요.

Part 2 학습 액티비티(Activities)

다양한 문제를 풀며 읽은 내용을 되돌아보고 어휘, 스토리 구조, 주요 문장 등을 다집니다.
문제 구성: Word Check • Story Check • Sentence Check • Story Map

Disney · PIXAR
Story Collection 2

Practice
Book

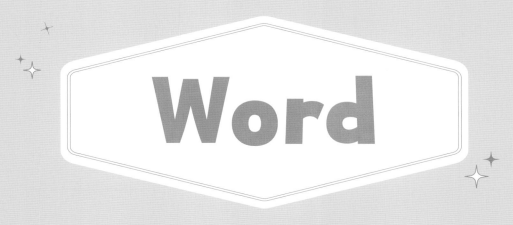

Word

Practice

FROZEN

중요 단어를 연습하고, 내가 찾은 단어도 기록해 보세요.

p.12~13

kingdom	몡 왕국
arrive	통 도착하다
inside	전 ~의 안에
magical	형 마법의
power	몡 힘
create	통 만들어내다
delighted	형 아주 즐거워하는

p.14~15

accidentally	부 우연히, 실수로
hurt	hurt(다치게 하다)의 과거형
rush	통 서둘러 보내다
cure	통 치유하다
memory	몡 기억
fear	통 ~를 두려워하다 몡 두려움
glove	몡 장갑

p.16-17

away	用 떨어져, 떨어진 곳에	
miss	통 그리워하다	
without	전 ~없이	
take over	~를 이어받다, 인수하다	
terrified	형 무서워하는	
lose	통 잃다	
front	명 앞쪽	

p.18-19

excited	형 신이 난	
especially	用 특히	
fall	통 빠지다, 떨어지다	
gather	통 모으다	
courage	명 용기	
take off	벗다	
successfully	用 성공적으로	

p.20—21

marry	통 결혼하다
forbade	forbid(금지하다)의 과거형
pull off	~을 벗기다
upset	형 속상한
expose	통 드러내다, 노출시키다
cover	통 가리다, 덮다
flee	통 도망치다

p.22—23

fault	명 잘못
reveal	통 (비밀 등을) 드러내다
find	통 찾다
hire	통 고용하다
alive	형 살아 있는
remember	통 기억하다
led	lead(이끌다)의 과거형, 과거분사

p.24-25

alone 형 부 혼자

free 형 자유로운

whatever 대 ~한 어떤[모든] 것

built build(짓다)의 과거형, 과거분사

palace 명 궁전

p.26-27

beg 동 애원하다

frozen 형 얼어붙은

control 동 조절하다, 통제하다

giant 형 거대한

p.28-29

turn 동 바뀌다, 변하다

troll 명 (북유럽신화) 난쟁이

advise 동 충고하다, 조언하다

thaw 동 녹이다

quickly 부 빨리, 빠르게

head	통 ~로 향하다	
✏️		
refuse `p.30-31`	통 거절하다	
plan	명 계획 통 계획을 세우다	
realize	통 깨닫다	
return	통 돌아오다	
danger	명 위험	
have to	~해야 한다	
✏️		
save `p.32-34`	통 구하다	
act	명 행동 통 행동하다	
between	전 사이에, 중간에	
melt	통 녹다, 녹이다	
became	become(~이 되다)의 과거형	
learn	통 ~을 알게 되다	
key	명 열쇠, 핵심	

FINDING NEMO

중요 단어를 연습하고, 내가 찾은 단어도 기록해 보세요.

p.40-41

most	때 대부분
above	전 ~위에
underwater	부 물속에
scared	형 무서워하는
always	부 항상
close	형 가까운 동 닫다
tuck	동 (작은 공간에) 집어넣다

p.42-43

excited	형 신이 난
on the way	부 도중에
spotted	형 점무늬가 있는
striped	형 줄무늬가 있는
angry	형 화난

p.44-45

| swim | 동 헤엄치다 |
| deep | 형 깊은 |

chase after	~을 쫓다	
embarrass	통 당황하게 만들다	
surface	명 수면, 표면	
ocean	명 바다, 대양	
touch	통 만지다, 건드리다	

p.46-47

caught	catch(잡다)의 과거형, 과거분사	
cry	통 소리치다, 울다	
take away	치우다, 제거하다	
sped	speed(빨리 가다)의 과거형, 과거분사	
disappear	통 사라지다	
give up	포기하다	
find	통 찾다	

p.48-49

look for	~을 찾다	
sort	명 종류	

8

push	동 밀다	
bump	동 부딪치다	
friendly	형 친절한	
see if	~인지 확인하다	
silly	형 어리석은	
✏️		

p.50–51

thought	think(생각하다)의 과거형, 과거분사	
invite	동 초대하다	
try	동 노력하다 명 시도	
luckily	부 다행스럽게도	
✏️		

p.52–53

search for	~를 찾다	
diver	명 잠수부	
mean	형 못된	
address	명 주소	
repeat	동 반복하다	

over and over	반복해서

p.54—55

funny	휑 웃긴, 재미있는
shape	똉 모양
point toward	~쪽을 가리키다
ride	똉 타기 툉 타다
news	똉 소식
spread	툉 퍼지다, 퍼뜨리다

p.56—57

heard	hear(듣다)의 과거형
escape	툉 탈출하다
fish tank	똉 수조
trap	툉 가두다 똉 덫
pride	똉 자랑스러움, 자부심
brave	휑 용감한

p.58-59

swallow 통 삼키다

worry 통 걱정하다

right 형 옳은, 올바른

in fact 사실

way 명 방법, 방식

grab 통 움켜잡다, 붙잡다

save 통 구하다

p.60-62

never 부 결코 ~않다

found find(찾다)의 과거형, 과거분사

overjoyed 형 매우 기뻐하는

finally 부 마침내

return 통 돌아오다

both 대 둘 다

hero 명 영웅

MONSTERS UNIVERSITY

중요 단어를 연습하고, 내가 찾은 단어도 기록해 보세요.

p.68-69

monster	명 괴물
scary	형 무서운
plan	명 계획 동 계획을 세우다
greatest	형 가장 대단한, 엄청난
first	형 첫 번째의
scare	동 겁주다 명 겁주기, 놀람
university	명 대학

p.70-71

serious	형 진지한
except	전 ~을 제외하고
get along	사이 좋게 지내다
thought	think(생각하다)의 과거형, 과거분사
lazy	형 게으른
prove	동 입증하다
wrong	형 틀린, 잘못된

p.72-73

work 통 일하다, 작업하다

hard 부 열심히, 힘껏

matter 통 문제가 되다

fight 통 분투하다, 싸우다

fail 통 (시험에) 떨어지다, 낙제하다

p.74-75

kick out of ~에서 쫓아내다

become 통 ~이 되다

ready 형 준비가 된

give up 포기하다

have to ~ 해야 한다

compete 통 경쟁하다, (시합에) 참가하다

join 통 가입하다, 합류하다

p.76-77

enough 부 충분히

get back 돌아오다

win	통 이기다	
least	부 가장 덜(little의 최상급)	
campus	명 교정, 캠퍼스	
look like	~처럼 보이다	
hairy	형 털이 많은	
held	hold(열다, 개최하다)의 과거형	

p.78-79

sewer	명 하수관	
beat	통 이기다	
last	부 맨 끝에, 마지막에	
cheat	통 속이다, 부정행위를 하다	
still	부 아직도	

p.80-81

sneak	통 살금살금 가다	
librarian	명 사서	
argue	통 다투다, 언쟁을 하다	

grab	통 붙잡다, 움켜잡다	
chance	명 기회, 가능성	
alike	형 (아주) 비슷한	
realize	통 깨닫다	

pay off	성과를 올리다	
eliminate	통 탈락시키다	
do better	더 잘하다	
pretend	통 ~인 체하다	
vanish	통 사라지다	
flat	형 납작한	
ceiling	명 천장	

| 🖉 | | |

p.84–85

practice	통 연습하다	
worried	형 걱정하는	
thrilled	형 아주 신이 난	

scream	몡 비명 통 비명을 지르다	
mad	휑 매우 화가 난	
believe	통 생각하다, ~라고 믿다	
🖉		

p.86–87

decide	통 결정하다	
forbidden	휑 금지된	
dangerous	휑 위험한	
follow	통 (~의 뒤를) 따라가다	
got trapped	갇히다	
enormous	휑 막대한, 거대한	
🖉		

p.88–90

come up with	(해답을) 찾아내다	
ranger	몡 경비 대원	
powerful	휑 강력한	
happen	통 발생하다	
as long as	~하는 한	

ENCANTO

중요 단어를 연습하고, 내가 찾은 단어도 기록해 보세요.

p.96-97

village 명 마을

glow 동 빛나다

shone shine(반짝이다)의 과거형, 과거분사

magic 명 마법

wonder 명 경이로운 것

p.98-99

gift 명 재능, 선물

heal 동 치유하다

strength 명 힘

grow 동 자라다

communicate 동 의사소통을 하다

future 명 미래

p.100-101

find out 알아내다, 알게 되다

knob 명 (문·서랍에 달린) 손잡이

go away 사라지다

special	형 특별한
worthy	형 가치가 있는
🖉	

p.102–103

crack	통 금이 가다 명 금
shake	통 흔들리다, 흔들다
danger	명 위험
reason	명 이유
fix	통 수리하다
prove	통 입증하다
🖉	

p.104–105

left	leave(떠나다)의 과거형, 과거분사
vision	명 환상, 예지력
determined	형 단단히 결심한
endless	형 끝없는
piece	명 (깨어진) 조각
🖉	

p.106-107

reveal 图 (비밀 등을) 드러내다

mean 图 의미하다

ripple 图 잔물결을 이루다

passageway 명 복도, 통로

whole 형 모든, 전체의

p.108-109

believe 图 믿다

restore 图 회복시키다, 복구하다

doomed 형 불운한

pursue 图 뒤쫓다, 추적하다

chaos 명 혼란

embrace 图 포옹하다

p.110-111

annoyingly 부 짜증나게

light 명 빛

bright 부 밝게

disrupt	통 방해하다	
dying	die(죽다)의 현재분사	
revelation	명 드러냄, 폭로	
✏		

p.112-113

melt	통 녹다, 녹이다	
fade	통 점점 희미해지다	
effort	명 노력	
gone	형 다 쓴, 떠난	
crumble	통 허물어지다	
shook	shake(흔들다)의 과거형	
defeated	형 패배한	
✏		

p.114-115

wander	통 거닐다	
born	통 태어나다	
lost	lose(잃다)의 과거형, 과거분사	
pray	통 기도하다	

20

protect	图 보호하다	
repair	图 수리하다	
fear	图 두려움	
✏️		

p.116-117

miracle	图 기적	
miss	图 놓치다	
important	图 중요한	
head	图 ~로 향하다	
proudly	图 자랑스럽게	
bond	图 유대	
✏️		

p.118

rebuild	图 다시 세우다	
at last	마침내, 드디어	
place	图 놓다, 두다 图 장소	
work	图 작동하다	
✏️		

LUCA

중요 단어를 연습하고, 내가 찾은 단어도 기록해 보세요.

p.124~125

spend 통 (돈·시간을) 쓰다, 보내다

herd 통 (동물을) 몰다

surface 명 수면, 표면

forbidden 형 금지된

land 명 육지, 땅

p.126~127

treasure 명 보물

reach 통 ~에 이르다, 닿다

transform 통 바뀌다, 변형시키다

strange 형 낯선, 이상한

hideout 명 비밀 은신처

full 형 (~이) 가득한

thing 명 것, 물건

build 통 만들어내다

p.128~129

island 명 섬

22

kind	명 종류	
rode	ride(타다)의 과거형	
soar	통 날아오르다	
safe	형 안전한	
send	통 보내다	
left	leave(떠나다)의 과거형, 과거분사	

p.130–131

seaside	형 해변의	
unsure	형 의심스러워하는, 확신하지 못하는	
at first	처음에는	
perfect	형 완벽한	
race	명 경주	
prize	명 상, 상품	

p.132–133

fisherman	명 어부	
exchange	명 교환 통 교환하다	

fee	명 요금
fishy	형 수상한
bully	명 괴롭히는 사람 동 괴롭히다
vow	동 맹세하다 명 맹세
defeat	동 패배시키다
✎	

p.134-135

determined	형 단단히 결심한, 단호한
training	명 훈련, 교육
practice	동 연습하다
amazed	형 놀란
✎	

p.136-137

quiet	형 조용한
threw	throw(던지다)의 과거형
harpoon	명 작살
figure out	알아내다
danger	명 위험

24

truth	몡 사실, 진실	
✏️		
p.138–139 protect	동 보호하다	
risky	형 위험한	
hide	동 숨기다, 감추다	
wear	동 입다	
avoid	동 피하다	
complete	동 완료하다, 끝마치다	
pass	동 지나가다, 통과하다	
search for	~를 찾다	
✏️		
p.140–141 trouble	몡 곤란, 골칫거리	
crowd	몡 사람들, 군중	
trap	동 가두다 몡 덫	
✏️		
p.142–143 aim	몡 목표, 조준 동 겨누다	

crash	동 충돌하다 명 사고
injured	형 부상을 입은
nervous	형 불안한
step forward	도움을 제공하고 나서다
accept	동 받아들이다, 수락하다
past	전 지나서
🖉	

p.144-146

bought	buy(사다)의 과거형, 과거분사
gather	동 모으다
backyard	명 뒷마당
sold	sell(팔다)의 과거형, 과거분사
apart	부 (공간, 시간 상으로) 떨어져
friendship	명 우정
last	동 지속되다
forever	부 영원히
🖉	

26

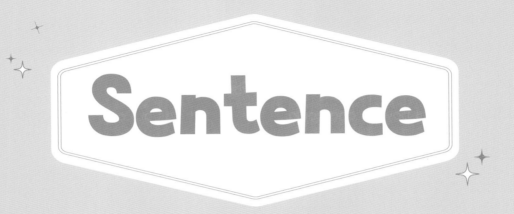

Sentence
Practice

FROZEN

빈칸에 알맞은 단어를 채워 문장을 완성하세요.

1 얼마 전에, 아렌델 왕국에 여름이 왔어요!

Not long ago in the [   ] of Arendelle, summer had arrived!

2 하지만 엘사와 안나 공주가 놀고 있는 성 안은 겨울이었어요.

But it was winter inside the [   ] where Princesses Elsa and Anna were playing.

3 엘사는 마법의 힘을 가지고 있어서 눈과 얼음으로 물건들을 만들어낼 수 있었어요!

Elsa had magical powers and could [   ] things out of snow and ice!

4 그녀는 올라프라는 이름의 눈사람을 만들었어요.

She made a [   ] named Olaf.

5 안나는 매우 즐거웠어요.

Anna was [   ].

6 그러다 엘사는 우연히 안나를 다치게 했어요.

Then Elsa accidentally [   ] Anna.

7 왕과 왕비는 두 소녀를 산 속에 사는 신비한 트롤들에게 급히 데려갔어요.

The king and queen [   ]ed both girls to the mystical trolls in the mountains.

8 트롤들은 엘사의 마법에 관한 안나의 기억을 바꾸어서 안나를 치료해 주었어요.

The trolls [   ]d Anna by changing her memories of Elsa's magic.

9 트롤들은 다른 사람들이 엘사의 힘을 두려워할 것이라고 경고했어요.

They [   ]ed that others would fear Elsa's power.

10 엘사가 힘을 통제하도록 돕기 위해, 엘사의 부모님은 그녀에게 장갑을 주었어요.

To help her [   ] it, Elsa's parents gave her gloves.

Word Box

kingdom	cure	create	control	delighted
명 왕국	통 병을 치유하다	통 만들어 내다	통 통제하다	형 아주 즐거워하는
hurt	rush	castle	caution	snowman
hurt(다치게 하다)의 과거형	통 급히 보내다	명 성	통 경고하다	명 눈사람

⑪ 성의 문은 닫혔고, 엘사는 안나와 떨어져 지냈어요. 엘사는 또 다시 안나를 다치게 하고 싶지 않았어요.

With the castle gates closed, Elsa stayed [   ] from Anna——she never wanted to hurt her again.

⑫ 하지만 엘사는 안나를 그리워했어요. 안나도 엘사가 보고 싶었어요.

But Elsa [   ]ed Anna. Anna missed Elsa.

⑬ 몇 년 후, 왕과 왕비는 바다에서 실종되었어요.

Years later, the king and queen were [   ] at sea.

⑭ 부모님을 잃은 두 공주는 점점 더 외롭게 자랐어요.

Without their parents, both princesses [   ] lonelier and lonelier.

⑮ 곧 엘사가 여왕의 자리를 물려받을 때가 되었어요.

Soon it was time for Elsa to take over as [   ].

⑯ 그녀는 두려웠어요. 장갑 없이는 사람들 앞에서 자신의 힘을 통제할 수 없을 것 같았거든요.

She was terrified that without her gloves, she might [   ] control of her powers in front of everyone!

⑰ 반면에 안나는 새로운 사람들을 만나서 신이 났어요. 특히 한스라는 이름의 왕자를요. 그들은 사랑에 빠졌어요!

Anna, on the other hand, was [   ] to meet new people——especially a prince named Hans. They fell in love!

⑱ 엘사는 자신의 모든 용기를 끌어 모아 장갑을 벗었어요. 그리고 성공적으로 아렌델 여왕의 자리에 올랐어요!

Elsa gathered all her courage to take off her gloves——and was successfully [   ]ed Queen of Arendelle!

⑲ 다시 장갑을 끼고, 엘사는 자랑스럽게 자신의 백성들 앞에 섰어요.

With her gloves back on, Elsa [   ] stood before her people.

Word Box

lost	miss	stay away	grew	proudly
형 행방불명된	동 그리워하다	떨어져 있다	grow(자라다)의 과거형	부 자랑스럽게
excited	lose	crown	queen	
형 신이 난	동 잃다	동 왕위에 앉히다	명 여왕	

20 하지만 안나가 한스와 결혼하고 싶다고 엘사에게 말하자, 엘사는 안 된다고 했어요.

But when Anna told Elsa that she wanted to marry Hans, Elsa [   ] it.

21 어떻게 안나는 방금 막 만난 남자와 결혼하고 싶을 수가 있을까요?

How could Anna want to marry a man she had only just [   ]?

22 실망한 안나는 언니를 말리려 하다가, 우연찮게 장갑 한 쪽을 잡아 당겨 벗기게 되었어요.

Frustrated, Anna tried to stop her sister and accidentally pulled off one [   ].

23 장갑 한 쪽이 없는 데다 안나 때문에 속상해서, 엘사는 실수로 그녀의 숨겨진 마법을 드러내고 말았어요.

Without her glove and upset with Anna, Elsa accidentally [   ]d her secret powers.

24 그녀의 손에서 얼음과 눈이 폭발하듯 뿜어져 나왔고 왕국을 덮어버렸어요.

Ice and snow [   ]ed from her hand, covering the kingdom.

25 엘사는 자신이 누군가를 다치게 하고 왕국을 파멸시킬까 두려워 도망쳤어요.

Fearing she might hurt someone and [   ] her kingdom, Elsa fled.

26 안나는 엘사의 마법이 드러난 것은 자신의 잘못이라고 생각했어요.

Anna thought it was her [   ] Elsa's powers had been revealed.

27 그녀는 언니를 찾으러 서둘러 달려갔어요.

She [   ]ed off to find her sister.

28 그녀는 크리스토프라는 이름의 산에 사는 남자를 그녀의 안내인으로 고용했어요.

She [   ]d a mountain man named Kristoff to be her guide.

29 때마침, 안나와 크리스토프는 올라프라는 이름의 눈사람을 찾았어요. 그는 살아 있었어요!

In time, Anna and Kristoff found a snowman named Olaf. He was [   ]!

Word Box

forbade forbid(금지하다)의 과거형	**expose** 통 드러내다	**glove** 명 장갑	**fault** 명 잘못	**hire** 통 고용하다
met meet(만나다)의 과거형	**ruin** 통 파멸시키다, 망치다	**rush** 통 서두르다	**blast** 통 폭발하다	**alive** 형 살아 있는

30 안나는 그를 기억해 냈어요. 언니와 함께 했던 행복한 시절도요. 올라프는 엘사에게로 가는 길을 안내했어요.

Anna remembered him——and the good times she had shared with her sister.
Olaf [   ] the way to Elsa.

31 엘사는 혼자만의 시간을 즐기고 있었어요. 이제 그녀는 자신이 원하는 것은 무엇이든 자유롭게 만들 수 있었어요.

Elsa was enjoying her time alone. Now she was free to create [   ] she wanted.

32 그녀는 얼음 궁전을 지었어요.

She built an ice [   ].

33 안나는 엘사에게 돌아가서 얼어붙은 왕국을 녹이자고 간청했어요. 하지만 엘사는 마법을 통제하지 못할까 봐 두려웠어요.

Anna begged Elsa to go home to thaw her [   ] kingdom. But Elsa feared she couldn't control her powers.

34 화가 나고 두려워서 엘사는 실수로 안나에게 얼어붙는 마법 주문을 걸어버렸어요. 그리고는 거대한 눈사람을 만들었어요.

Angry and afraid, Elsa accidentally cast a magic freezing [   ] on her little sister and then created a giant snowman.

35 안나와 크리스토프는 달렸어요. 올라프도 함께 달렸어요. 안나의 머리카락이 하얀색으로 변하기 시작했어요.

Anna and Kristoff ran. Olaf ran, too. Anna's hair began to [   ] white.

36 크리스토프는 그녀를 트롤에게 데려가 도움을 청했어요. 트롤들은 충고했어요. "오직 진실한 사랑에서 나온 행동만이 얼어붙은 심장을 녹일 수 있어요."

Kristoff led her to the trolls for help. The trolls advised, "Only an [   ] of true love can thaw a frozen heart."

37 안나는 진실한 사랑의 입맞춤을 위해 한스가 필요했어요!

Anna needed Hans for a true love's [   ]!

38 재빠르게, 크리스토프와 안나는 아렌델로 다시 향했어요.

Quickly, Kristoff and Anna [   ]ed back to Arendelle.

Word Box

whatever	led	frozen	head	spell
때 ~한 무엇이든	lead(안내하다)의 과거형	형 얼어붙은	통 ~로 향하다	명 주문
act	turn	kiss	palace	
명 행동, 행위	통 ~로 변하다	명 입맞춤	명 궁전	

39 안나가 한스를 찾아냈을 때, 그는 그녀에게 입맞추는 것을 거절했어요.

When Anna found Hans, he [   ]d to kiss her.

40 지금까지 내내 그의 계획은 왕국을 차지하는 것이었거든요.

His [   ] all along had been to take over the kingdom.

41 안나의 마음은 짓밟혔어요! 안나는 크리스토프가 자신을 사랑한다는 것을 깨달았어요!

Anna was [   ]ed! Anna realized that Kristoff loved her!

42 그녀는 그를 찾기 위해 자신의 모든 힘을 모았어요.

She needed all her [   ] to find him.

43 한편 엘사는 그녀의 왕국을 구하기 위해 아렌델로 돌아왔어요.

[   ], Elsa had returned to Arendelle to save her kingdom.

44 하지만 이제 그녀는 끔찍한 위험에 빠졌어요.

But now she was in terrible [   ].

45 안나가 한스를 보았을 때, 그녀는 무엇을 해야만 하는지 알았어요. 안나는 엘사를 구했어요.

When Anna saw Hans, she knew what she had to do. Anna [   ]d Elsa.

46 그것은 진실한 사랑에서 나온 행동이었어요. 자매 사이의 진실한 사랑이었죠.

It was an act of true love——true love [   ] two sisters.

47 곧 얼음이 녹았어요. 그리고 안나는 자신이 크리스토프를 사랑한다는 것을 깨달았어요.

Soon the ice [   ]ed. And Anna realized she was in love with Kristoff.

48 엘사에 대해 말하자면, 그녀는 다시 여왕이 되었어요. 자신의 마법을 통제할 수 있는 열쇠는 사랑이었다는 사실을 동생으로부터 배운 멋진 여왕이었답니다.

As for Elsa, she became queen again——a good queen who had learned from her sister that love was the [   ] to controlling her powers.

Word Box

crush	plan	meanwhile	strength	refuse
통 으스러뜨리다	명 계획	부 한편	명 힘	통 거절하다
between	**save**	**danger**	**melt**	**key**
전 ~사이의	통 구하다	명 위험	통 녹다	명 열쇠, 핵심

FINDING NEMO

빈칸에 알맞은 단어를 채워 문장을 완성하세요.

1 자, 이 책을 읽고 있는 여러분은 아마 대부분 바다보다 위에 살고 있겠지요. 하지만 다른 생명체들은 물속에 산답니다.

Now, most of you who are reading this book probably live [____] the sea... but others live underwater.

2 니모와 그의 아버지인 말린은 물속에 살았어요. 그들은 흰동가리였어요.

Nemo and his father, Marlin, lived underwater. They were [____].

3 그들은 흰동가리였기 때문에 작았어요. 하지만 다른 물고기들은 컸답니다!

[____] they were clownfish, they were small. But other fish were big!

4 말린은 큰 물고기가 무서웠어요. 그래서 니모를 늘 자신 가까이에 두었고, 그들의 작은 집 안으로 안전하게 들여보냈어요.

Marlin was scared of the big fish, so he always kept Nemo [____] to him, tucked safely inside their little home.

5 하지만 오늘은 니모가 학교에 가는 첫날이었어요!

But today was Nemo's [____] day of school!

6 그는 매우 신이 났어요.

He was very [____].

7 학교 가는 길에 그는 점무늬가 있는 물고기 한 마리와 줄무늬 물고기 한 마리를 보았어요.

On the way there he saw a [____] fish and a striped fish.

8 그는 화가 난 물고기와 행복한 물고기도 보았어요.

He saw [____] fish and happy fish.

9 과학 선생님인 레이 씨는 니모의 반 친구들을 현장 학습에 데려갔어요.

Mr. Ray, the science teacher, took Nemo's class on a [____] [____].

Word Box

excited	clownfish	above	close	first
형 신이 난	명 흰동가리	전 ~보다 위에	형 가까운	형 첫 번째의
because	field trip	angry	spotted	
접 ~때문에	명 현장 학습	형 화가 난	형 점무늬가 있는	

10 니모와 친구들은 몰래 빠져나와 바다 깊은 곳까지 헤엄쳐 갔어요.

Nemo and his friends _____ed away and swam to the really deep water.

11 말린이 니모를 쫓아와서 그를 꾸짖었어요!

Marlin chased after Nemo and _____ed him!

12 니모는 아빠가 친구들 앞에서 망신을 주어서 화가 났어요. 그래서 그는 바다의 수면을 향해 위로 헤엄쳐 올라갔어요. 그리고 배 한 척을 건드렸어요!

Nemo was angry that his father had _____ed him in front of his new friends so he swam and swam way up to the surface of the ocean until he touched a boat!

13 그러다가 니모가 잡혔어요!

Then Nemo got _____!

14 "아빠!" 니모가 외쳤어요. "니모!" 말린이 외쳤어요.

"Daddy!" _____ Nemo. "Nemo!" cried Marlin.

15 니모는 배에 실려 멀어져 갔어요.

Nemo was taken _____ in the boat.

16 말린은 아들을 구하려 했지만, 배는 너무나 빨리 지나갔고 결국 사라져 버렸어요.

Marlin tried to save his son, but the boat _____ away so fast it soon disappeared.

17 니모가 떠나버렸어요.

Nemo was _____.

18 하지만 말린은 포기하지 않았어요.

But Marlin would not _____ _____.

19 지금 그의 마음 속에는 니모를 찾는 것밖에 없었어요.

The only thing on his mind now was _____ing Nemo.

Word Box

sneak 통 몰래 빠져나오다	**embarrass** 통 부끄럽게 하다	**find** 통 찾아내다	**caught** catch(잡다)의 과거분사	**scold** 통 꾸짖다
gone 형 떠난	**sped** speed(빨리 가다)의 과거형	**away** 부 (멀리) 떨어져	**give up** 포기하다	**cried** cry(외치다)의 과거형

20 도움을 청할 곳을 찾아 말린은 온갖 종류의 물고기들에게 헤엄쳐 갔어요.

[_____]ing for help, Marlin swam into all sorts of fish.

21 그들은 말린을 밀고 또 거칠게 떠밀었어요.

They [_____]ed him and shoved him.

22 그들은 그에게 부딪쳐 왔어요.

They [_____]ed into him.

23 곧 말린은 한쪽으로 나가떨어졌어요.

Soon Marlin was [_____]ed aside.

24 도리라는 이름의 친절한 물고기가 말린이 괜찮은지 확인하러 헤엄쳐 왔어요.

One [_____] fish named Dory swam down to see if Marlin was okay.

25 그녀는 조금 어리석었고, 기억력이 안 좋았지만 기꺼이 말린을 도와주기로 했어요.

She was a little bit [_____], and she couldn't remember very much, but she was happy to help Marlin!

26 도리와 말린은 상어를 만났어요.

Together, Dory and Marlin met a [_____].

27 말린은 무서웠어요!

Marlin was [_____]!

28 하지만 도리는 그 상어가 참 친절하다고 생각했어요. 그들을 파티에 초대했거든요.

But Dory thought it was very nice of the shark to [_____] them to a party.

29 그 파티는 물고기를 먹지 않으려 노력하는 상어들을 위한 것이었어요.

The party was for sharks who were [_____]ing not to eat fish.

Word Box

bump	push	look for	knock	try
통 ~에 부딪치다	통 밀다	~을 찾다	통 (치거나 때려서) ~한 상태가 되게 하다	통 노력하다
invite	shark	scared	silly	friendly
통 초대하다	명 상어	형 겁먹은	형 어리석은	형 친절한

30 다행히 상어들은 말린과 도리를 먹지 않았어요.

_____, they did not eat Marlin and Dory.

31 말린은 니모를 계속 찾아다녔어요.

Marlin kept _____ing for Nemo.

32 말린과 도리는 니모를 데려간 잠수부의 스쿠버 마스크를 발견했어요.

He and Dory found a _____ _____ that belonged to the diver who had taken Nemo.

33 그들은 그것을 가지러 매우 깊고 감감한 곳까지 헤엄쳐 내려갔어요. 그리고 그들은 한 줄기 빛을 보았어요.

They swam down into a very deep, _____ place to get it. Then they saw a light.

34 그 빛은 사나운 아귀에게 붙어 있었어요!

The light was _____ed to a mean anglerfish!

35 하지만 그 불빛은 도리가 마스크에 적힌 주소를 읽는 데 도움이 되었어요.

But it helped Dory read an _____ written on the mask.

36 그리곤 두 친구들은 아귀가 그들을 잡아 먹기 전에 도망쳤어요!

Then the two friends swam away _____ the anglerfish could eat them!

37 이제 말린은 어디서 니모를 찾아야 할지 알게 되었어요. 시드니 왈라비 웨이 42번가예요.

Now Marlin _____ where to find Nemo: 42 Wallaby Way, Sydney.

38 도리는 너무나 신이 나서 그 주소를 계속해서 되풀이했어요.

Dory was so excited that she _____ed the address over and over and over.

39 말린과 도리는 배불뚝치를 몇 마리를 만났어요.

Next Marlin and Dory met some _____.

Word Box

before 젭 ~하기 전에	**address** 몡 주소	**moonfish** 몡 배불뚝치	**repeat** 통 되풀이하다	**knew** know(알다)의 과거형
luckily 뷔 다행히도	**search** 통 찾아보다	**attach** 통 붙이다	**dark** 혱 감감한	**scuba mask** 몡 (물안경처럼 생긴) 스쿠버 마스크

40 배불뚝치들은 재미있는 모양을 만들었어요.

The moonfish made [_____] shapes.

41 그들은 시드니 왈라비 웨이 42번가로 가는 방향을 가리켰어요.

They [_____]ed toward 42 Wallaby Way, Sydney.

42 몇몇 친절한 거북이들이 말린과 도리를 태워줬어요.

Some friendly turtles gave Marlin and Dory a [_____].

43 말린은 니모를 찾고 있는 사연을 말했고, 그 소식은 온 바다에 퍼졌어요!

Marlin told the story of his search for Nemo, and the news [_____] across the ocean!

44 심지어 니모까지도 시드니 왈라비 웨이 42번가에서 그 이야기를 듣게 되었답니다! 그는 매우 신이 났어요!

Even Nemo [_____] about it at 42 Wallaby Way, Sydney. He was very excited!

45 그는 자신이 갇혀 있는 수조에서 탈출하고 싶었어요.

He wanted to escape from the fish tank where he was [_____]ped.

46 니모의 새 친구들도 신이 났어요. 꼬마 흰동가리의 마음은 자랑스러움으로 터질 듯했어요.

Nemo's new friends were excited, too. The little clownfish was bursting with [_____].

47 그에겐 바다에서 최고로 용감한 아빠가 있었던 거예요!

He had the [_____] dad in the sea!

48 그런데 갑자기 고래 한 마리가 말린과 도리를 삼켜버렸어요!

Then a whale [_____]ed Marlin and Dory!

49 도리는 말린에게 걱정할 필요 없다고 말했어요. 그리고 도리의 말이 맞았어요.

Dory told Marlin he didn't need to [_____]. And she was right.

Word Box

funny	spread	point	give a ride	heard
형 재미있는	spread(퍼지다)의 과거형	동 가리키다	태워주다	hear(듣다)의 과거형
swallow	pride	bravest	trap	worry
동 삼키다	명 자랑스러움, 자부심	brave(용감한)의 최상급	동 가두다	동 걱정하다

50 고래는 시드니 왈라비 웨이 42번가에 닿을 수 있을 만큼 가까운 곳까지 그들을 데려다 주었어요.

The [   ] took them as close as he could get to 42 Wallaby Way, Sydney.

51 사실 고래는 그들을 시드니 항구까지 쭉 데려다 준 것이었어요!

In fact, he took them all the way to Sydney [   ]!

52 마지막으로, 나이젤이라는 이름의 펠리컨 한 마리가 말린과 도리를 도와 시드니 왈라비 웨이 42번가에 곧장 가도록 해주었어요.

At last a [   ] named Nigel helped Marlin and Dory go straight to 42 Wallaby Way, Sydney.

53 하지만 너무 늦었어요. 한 어린 소녀가 니모를 움켜잡았어요.

But it was too [   ]. A little girl had grabbed Nemo.

54 말린은 도리를 구할 수 없었어요! 말린은 슬펐어요.

Marlin couldn't [   ] him! Marlin was sad.

55 그는 아들을 다시는 볼 수 없을 거라 생각했어요.

He [   ] he would never see his son again.

56 하지만 니모는 탈출했어요! 도리가 그를 발견했어요.

But Nemo had [   ]d! Dory found him.

57 아버지와 아들은 몹시 기뻤어요.

Father and son were [   ].

58 그리고 그들이 마침내 집에 돌아왔을 때, 니모와 말린은 영웅이 되어 있었어요.

And when they finally [   ]ed home, both Nemo and Marlin were heroes.

Word Box

escape	whale	harbor	pelican	late
통 탈출하다	명 고래	명 항구	명 펠리컨	형 늦은
return	save	overjoyed	thought	
통 돌아오다	통 구하다	형 매우 기뻐하는	think(생각하다)의 과거형	

MONSTERS UNIVERSITY

빈칸에 알맞은 단어를 채워 문장을 완성하세요.

1 마이크는 작았어요. 그리고 녹색이었고 동그랬어요.

Mike was [   ]. And green. And round.

2 몇몇 몬스터들은 그가 별로 무섭지 않다고 말하곤 했어요.

Some monsters would say he wasn't very [   ].

3 하지만 마이크에게는 계획이 있었어요. 커다란 계획들이요.

But Mike had [   ]s, big plans.

4 그는 언젠가 세계가 처음 보는 가장 위대한 겁주기 선수가 되려 했어요!

Someday he was going to be the [   ] Scarer the world had ever seen!

5 그리고 그 첫번째 단계는? 몬스터 대학교에서 겁주는 방법을 배우는 것이었어요!

And the first step? Learning how to [   ] at Monsters University!

6 마이크는 진지한 학생이었어요. 그는 공부하기를 좋아했어요. 그는 모든 수업들을 좋아했어요.

Mike was a [   ] student. He liked studying. He liked his classes.

7 사실 마이크는 학교에 관한 모든 것을 좋아했어요. 설리만 제외하고요.

In fact, he liked everything about school... [   ] Sulley.

8 설리는 마이크의 겁주기 수업에 있는 또 다른 학생이었어요.

Sulley was another student in Mike's Scaring [   ].

9 마이크와 설리는 잘 어울리지 못했어요.

Mike and Sulley just didn't get [   ].

10 마이크는 설리가 게으르다고 생각했어요.

Mike thought Sulley was [   ].

Word Box

plan 명 계획	**scare** 통 겁을 주다	**small** 형 작은	**greatest** 형 가장 위대한	**class** 명 수업
get along 사이좋게 지내다	**except** 전 ~을 제외하고	**lazy** 형 게으른	**serious** 형 진지한	**scary** 형 무서운

11 설리는 마이크가 너무 작고 귀여워서 겁을 줄 수 없을 것이라 생각했어요.

Sulley thought Mike was too [little] and cute to be scary.

12 마이크는 설리가 틀렸다는 것을 빨리 증명하고 싶었어요!

Mike couldn't wait to prove Sulley [wrong]!

13 마이크는 열심히 노력했어요. 설리는 놀았어요.

Mike worked [hard]. Sulley played.

14 마이크는 공부했어요. 설리는 파티에 갔어요.

Mike studied. Sulley [went] to parties.

15 마이크는 A학점을 받았어요. 설리는 C학점을 받았어요.

Mike [got] As. Sulley got Cs.

16 하지만 그것은 문제되지 않았어요.

But it didn't [matter].

17 중요한 시험 도중에 마이크와 설리는 싸움을 했어요.

During a big test, Mike and Sulley got into a [fight].

18 두 몬스터 모두 낙제했어요!

Both monsters [fail]ed!

19 설리와 마이크는 겁주기 수업에서 쫓겨났어요.

Sulley and Mike were [kick out of]ed out of Scaring class.

20 이제 그 둘은 어떻게 위대한 겁주기 선수가 될 수 있을까요?

How would they [become] great Scarers now?

Word Box

went	wrong	fail	little	got
go(가다)의 과거형	형 틀린	통 낙제하다	형 작은, 어린	get(받다)의 과거형
matter	**become**	**hard**	**kick out of**	**fight**
통 문제가 되다	통 ~이 되다	부 열심히	~에서 쫓아내다	명 싸움

40

21 마이크는 그의 꿈을 포기할 준비가 되어 있지 않았어요.

Mike wasn't ready to [   ] [   ] his dream.

22 그는 겁주기 대회 포스터를 보았어요.

He saw a [   ] for the Scare Games.

23 겁주기 대회에서 우승하면 그가 무섭다는 게 증명될 것이었어요.

Winning the Scare Games would [   ] he was scary.

24 그러면 학교는 그가 다시 겁주기 수업으로 돌아갈 수 있게 해 줄 거예요!

Then the university would have to [   ] him back into Scaring class!

25 문제가 하나 있었어요.

There was one [   ].

26 대회에 참가하기 위해 마이크는 학교의 팀들 중 한 곳에 들어가야만 했어요.

To [   ] in the games, Mike had to join one of the school's teams.

27 으르렁 히어로 팀은 마이크가 그들의 팀원이 될 정도로 충분히 무섭지 않다고 생각했어요.

The Roar Omega Roars didn't think Mike was scary [   ] to be a member of their team.

28 하지만 울지 마 까꿍 팀은 그를 좋아했어요. 마이크를 포함하여 울지 마 까꿍팀은 5명의 팀원을 가지게 되었어요.

But the Oozma Kappas liked him. [   ] Mike, the Oozma Kappas had five monsters.

29 대회에 참가하려면 총 6명의 팀원이 필요했어요.

They [   ]ed six to be in the games.

30 그 밖에 다른 누가 팀원이 되고 싶어 했을까요?

Did anyone [   ] want to join?

Word Box

prove 통 증명하다	poster 명 포스터	catch 명 문제점	let 통 ~하게 하다	give up 포기하다
compete 통 (경기 등에) 참가하다	need 통 필요로 하다	with 전 ~를 포함하여	enough 부 충분히	else 부 그 밖의, 다른

31 설리요! 그도 겁주기 수업에 다시 돌아가고 싶었거든요!

Sulley did! He wanted to [   ] [   ] into Scaring class, too!

32 하지만 울지 마 까꿍 팀은 겁주기 대회에서 어떻게 우승할 수 있을까요?

But how could the Oozma Kappas ever [   ] the Scare Games?

33 그들은 캠퍼스에서 가장 덜 무서운 몬스터들이었거든요.

They were the [   ] scary monsters on campus.

34 오직 설리만 진짜 겁주기 선수처럼 보였어요.

Only Sulley looked [   ] a real Scarer.

35 곧 겁주기 대회가 시작됐어요.

Soon the Scare Games [   ].

36 첫 번째 경기는 학교 지하에 있는 하수도에서 열렸어요.

The first event was [   ] underground in the school's sewer.

37 설리와 마이크는 둘 다 우승하고 싶었어요.

Sulley and Mike [   ] wanted to win.

38 둘은 서로를 이기기 위해 너무 열심히 노력한 바람에, 울지 마 까꿍 팀의 팀원들을 뒤에 둔 채 앞서가고 말았어요.

They were trying so hard to beat each other that they left the [   ] of the OKs behind.

39 울지 마 까꿍 팀은 맨 마지막으로 들어왔어요.

Their team came in [   ].

40 하지만 다른 한 팀이 부정행위로 쫓겨났어요.

But another team was kicked out for [   ].

Word Box

began	**win**	**last**	**look like**	**get back**
begin(시작하다)의 과거형	통 이기다	부 맨 마지막으로	~처럼 보이다	돌아오다
held	**rest**	**both**	**least**	**cheating**
hold(열다, 개최하다)의 과거형	명 나머지	대 둘 다	형 가장 덜, 최소의	명 부정 행위

㊶ 울지 마 까꿍 팀은 아직 달리는 중이었고요!

The Oozma Kappas were still in the [   ]!

㊷ 두 번째 경기에서 몬스터들은 사서를 살금살금 지나쳐 깃발을 가져와야 했어요.

For the second event, the monsters needed to [   ] past the librarian to get their flag.

㊸ 마이크와 설리가 우승하기 위한 방법에 대해 논쟁하는 동안, 울지 마 까꿍의 나머지 팀원들은 함께 행동했어요.

While Mike and Sulley [   ]d about the best way to win, the other Oozma Kappas worked together.

㊹ 돈, 테리와 테리, 그리고 아트는 사서의 주의를 딴 데로 돌렸고, 그 사이에 스퀴시가 깃발을 움켜잡았어요.

Don, Terri, Terry, and Art [   ]ed the librarian while Squishy grabbed the flag!

㊺ 그 후, 마이크는 팀으로 협동할 때 우승할 가능성이 더 높아진다는 사실을 깨달았어요.

After that, Mike realized that if they worked as a team, they'd have a better [   ] of winning.

㊻ 그러나 설리는 울지 마 까꿍 팀이 겁주기 대회에서 우승할 정도로 충분히 무서워질 수 있을 것이라 믿지 않았어요.

But Sulley didn't [   ] the Oozma Kappas could ever be scary enough to win the Scare Games.

㊼ 그래서 마이크는 그들을 데리고 몬스터 주식회사로 현장 학습을 갔어요.

So Mike took them on a [   ] [   ] to Monsters, Inc.

㊽ 세계에서 가장 훌륭한 겁주기 선수들이 그곳에서 일하고 있었어요. 그들은 비슷한 구석이 한 군데도 없었어요!

The greatest Scarers in the world worked there—and they looked nothing [   ]!

㊾ 무서워 보이는 방법은 하나만 있는 것이 아니라는 사실을 설리는 깨달았어요.

Sulley realized there wasn't just one [   ] to be scary.

㊿ 울지 마 까꿍 팀은 팀으로서 힘을 모았어요.

The Oozma Kappas were coming [   ] as a team.

Word Box

argue 통 논쟁하다	sneak 통 살금살금 가다	running 명 달리기	chance 명 가능성	distract 통 주의를 딴 데로 돌리다
alike 형 비슷한	field trip 명 현장 학습	believe 통 믿다	way 명 방법	come together 힘을 합치다

51 그들의 노력은 성공적이었어요.

And their hard work [   ] off.

52 다른 팀들이 차례대로 탈락했고, 울지 마 까꿍 팀은 그 어느 때보다도 더 잘 해내고 있었어요!

One by one, the other teams were getting [   ]d from the Scare Games——and the Oozma Kappas were doing better than ever!

53 '숨어서 살금살금 들어가기' 경기에서 설리는 양탄자인 척했어요.

In the Hide-and-Sneak event, Sulley [   ]ed to be a rug.

54 마이크는 배경 속으로 사라지다시피 해서 모습을 감추었어요.

Mike nearly [   ]ed into the background.

55 하지만 최고로 잘한 몬스터는 돈이었어요. 그는 천장에 납작하게 붙어버렸답니다!

But the star was Don. He stuck himself [   ] against the ceiling!

56 마침내 단 두 팀만 남았어요. 으르렁 히어로 팀과 울지 마 까꿍 팀이었죠.

[   ] only two teams were left——the RORs and the OKs.

57 마지막 경기는 겁주기였어요! 경기 전 날, 마이크와 설리는 계속 연습했어요.

The last event? Scaring! The night before, Mike and Sulley [   ]d and practiced.

58 하지만 설리는 걱정되었어요. 마이크는 충분히 무서워졌을까요?

Still, Sulley was [   ]. Was Mike scary enough?

59 설리는 모험을 하지 않기로 했어요.

Sulley wasn't taking any [   ].

60 그는 겁주기 방 안의 기계 설정을 마이크에게 유리하도록 바꿨어요.

He changed the [   ]s in the scare room to make it easier for Mike.

Word Box

setting	**eliminate**	**pretend**	**take chances**	**vanish**
명 설정, 환경	통 탈락시키다	통 ~인 체하다	모험을 하다, 위험을 무릅쓰다	통 사라지다
practice	**finally**	**worried**	**paid off**	**flat**
통 연습하다	부 마침내	형 걱정하는	pay off(성공하다)의 과거형	형 평평한, 납작한

44

61 마이크는 경기에서 엄청나게 큰 비명 소리를 듣고 아주 흥분했어요.

Mike was [_____] to get a huge scream in the event.

62 그리고 그는 설리가 속임수를 썼다는 사실을 알게 됐어요! 마이크는 매우 화가 났어요.

Then he found out that Sulley had cheated! Mike was [_____].

63 시간이 그렇게 흘렀는데도, 설리는 아직도 그를 믿지 않았던 거예요.

After all this time, Sulley [_____] didn't believe in him.

64 마이크는 자신이 얼마나 무서운지를 모두에게 보여주기로 결심했어요.

Mike [_____]ed to show everyone how scary he was.

65 그는 진짜 아이를 겁주기로 결심했어요.

He'd scare a [_____] child.

66 그는 금지된 문을 살금살금 통과해 인간 세상으로 들어갔어요.

He snuck through a [_____] door and into the human world.

67 그는 캠핑 온 아이들의 방 안에 들어왔어요.

He found himself in a room of [_____]s.

68 마이크는 그가 가장 잘 하는 겁주기를 시도했어요. "으르렁!" 하지만 아이들은 그냥 웃기만 했어요.

Mike [_____] out his best scare—— "ROAR!" But the kids just smiled.

69 설리는 속임수를 써서 미안했고, 마이크가 걱정되었어요.

Sulley was [_____] for cheating——and he was worried about Mike.

70 인간들은 위험했거든요! 그래서 설리는 마이크의 뒤를 따라갔어요.

Humans were dangerous! So Sulley [_____]ed him.

Word Box

thrilled	sorry	still	real	decide
형 아주 흥분한	형 미안한	부 아직도	형 진짜의	동 결심하다
mad	**camper**	**tried**	**forbidden**	**follow**
형 매우 화가 난	명 캠핑객	try(시도하다)의 과거형	형 금지된	동 따라가다

71 하지만 그들은 인간 세계에 갇혀버렸어요.

But they both got [   ]ped in the human world.

72 오직 한 가지, 엄청나게 큰 비명 소리만이 그들을 탈출시켜 줄 수 있었어요.

Only one thing could get them out——an [   ] scream.

73 큰 비명은 충분한 에너지를 만들어서 몬스터 대학교로 통하는 문을 열어 줄 것이었어요.

It would make enough [   ] to open the door back to Monsters University!

74 마이크와 설리는 함께 계획을 세워 캠프 경비원들을 놀라게 하기로 했어요.

Together, Mike and Sulley came up with a plan that would scare the pants off the camp [   ]s.

75 무서움에서 나온 비명 에너지를 이용해, 그들은 몬스터 세계로 돌아가는 방법을 찾아냈어요.

Using scream energy from the scare, they [   ] their way back to the monster world.

76 처음 만났을 때 마이크와 설리는 서로 좋아하지 않았어요.

Mike and Sulley hadn't liked [   ] [   ] when they first met.

77 하지만 이제 그들은 친구였어요. 그리고 강력한 한 팀이 되었죠.

But now they were friends. And they made a [   ] team.

78 서로 함께 붙어있는 한, 다음에 어떤 일이 일어나도 괜찮을 거라는 사실을 알게 되었어요.

They knew that [   ] happened next, they'd be okay——as long as they stuck together.

Word Box

ranger	enormous	energy	trap
명 경비 대원	형 엄청나게 큰	명 에너지	통 가두다
each other	found	powerful	whatever
서로	find(찾다)의 과거형	형 강력한	대 무엇이든

ENCANTO

빈칸에 알맞은 단어를 채워 문장을 완성하세요.

1 황무지 깊은 곳의 작은 마을에 꺼지지 않는 초가 밝게 빛나고 있었어요.

In a small village deep in the wilderness, an ever-glowing [＿＿＿＿] shone brightly.

2 그것의 마법은 아주 강력해서 경이로운 장소를 탄생시켰어요. 바로 엔칸토였죠!

Its magic was so powerful, a place of [＿＿＿＿] was born... an Encanto!

3 마드리갈 가족은 엔칸토에 있는 집에서 살았고 그 집을 카시타라고 불렀어요.

The Madrigal family lived there in a home they [＿＿＿＿]ed Casita.

4 마법은 마드리갈 가족 모두에게 특별한 재능을 주어 축복했어요.

The magic blessed all the Madrigals with special [＿＿＿＿]s.

5 훌리에타는 음식으로 사람들을 치유해줄 수 있었어요. 루이사는 힘이 엄청나게 셌어요.

Julieta could [＿＿＿＿] people with food. Luisa had superstrength.

6 이사벨라는 꽃들을 자라게 할 수 있었어요. 안토니오는 동물들과 의사소통 할 수 있었어요.

Isabela could make flowers grow. Antonio could [＿＿＿＿] with animals.

7 그리고 브루노는 미래를 볼 수 있었어요. 하지만 아무도 브루노에 관해서는 이야기하지 않았어요.

And Bruno could see the future. But [＿＿＿＿] talked about Bruno.

8 그는 여러 해 전에 떠나 버렸거든요.

He had been [＿＿＿＿] for many years.

9 미라벨이 5살이 되었을 때, 그녀는 특별한 파티 드레스를 입게 되었어요!

When Mirabel was five years old, she got to wear her special party [＿＿＿＿]!

10 그녀와 아부엘라 알마는 미라벨의 재능이 무엇인지 알아내기 위해 흥분한 상태였어요.

She and Abuela Alma were so excited to [＿＿＿＿] out what her gift was!

Word Box

candle	gift	wonder	call	heal
명 초, 양초	명 재능	명 경이로운 것	동 ~라고 부르다	동 치유하다
communicate	nobody	find out	gone	dress
동 의사소통을 하다	대 아무도(~하지 않다)	알아내다	형 떠난	명 드레스

11 하지만 미라벨이 빛나는 문의 손잡이에 손을 대자 마법은 사라졌어요!

But when Mirabel touched the _____ of her glowing door... the magic went away!

12 마드리갈 가족 중에 유일하게 그녀만이 재능이 없었어요.

She was the only Madrigal _____ a gift.

13 이 사실은 미라벨이 스스로를 충분히 특별하지 않고 충분히 가치도 없는 사람이라고 느끼게 만들었어요.

This made her feel like she wasn't special enough or _____ enough.

14 어느 날, 미라벨이 15살이 되었을 때, 카시타에 금이 가기 시작했어요. 그것은 흔들리기 시작했어요.

One day, when Mirabel was fifteen, Casita started to crack. It began to _____ .

15 "집이 위험해!" 미라벨이 외쳤어요. 갑자기 그녀에게 생각이 떠올랐어요.

"The house is in danger!" Mirabel cried. _____ , she had an idea.

16 만약 금이 간 이유를 알아내서 고친다면, 이것으로 자신이 특별하다는 것을 증명할 수 있을 거예요!

If she found the reason for the cracks, she could fix them and _____ she was special!

17 미라벨은 갈라진 금을 따라 곧장 마법의 초로 향했어요.

Mirabel _____ ed the cracks straight to the magical candle.

18 그녀의 언니인 루이사가 브루노에 대해 말해줬어요. 그는 미래에 관한 마지막 예지에서 본 것 때문에 떠났다는 것을요.

Her sister Luisa told her that Bruno left the Encanto because of what he saw in his last _____ about the future.

19 그것이 갈라진 금들과 관련이 있을 수도 있을까요?

Could it have something to do with the _____ s?

Word Box

without	knob	crack	worthy	suddenly
전 ~없이	명 손잡이	명 금, 깨진 틈	형 가치 있는	부 갑자기
follow	prove	shake	vision	
통 따라가다	통 증명하다	통 흔들리다	명 예지력	

48

20 미라벨은 브루노의 예지 동굴을 찾아내기로 결심했어요.

Mirabel was _____ to find Bruno's vision cave.

21 끝없는 계단을 오른 후에, 그녀는 마침내 그의 방 안에 도착했어요.

After climbing endless _____s, she was finally inside his room.

22 그곳에서 그녀는 밝게 빛나고 있는 브루노의 깨어진 예지 조각들을 찾아냈어요.

There, she found glowing _____s of his broken vision.

23 미라벨은 브루노의 예지 조각들을 모두 끼워 맞췄어요.

Mirabel put all the pieces of Bruno's vision _____.

24 퍼즐은 무너진 카시타의 모습을 드러냈는데, 그 한가운데에 미라벨이 있었어요! 이것은 무슨 뜻일까요?

The puzzle _____ed a destroyed Casita, and in the middle was MIRABEL!
What did it mean?

25 그러는 사이, 더 많은 금들이 집 사이로 잔물결처럼 퍼져 나가기 시작했어요.

Meanwhile, more cracks started to _____ through the house.

26 미라벨에게는 시간이 없었어요!

Mirabel was running out of _____!

27 그녀는 벽 안에 있는 비밀 통로를 발견했어요.

She discovered a secret _____ inside the walls.

28 그리고 그곳에서 브루노를 찾았어요! 그는 그동안 내내 그곳에서 살고 있었던 거예요!

And there she found Bruno! He had been _____ there the whole while!

29 미라벨은 브루노에게 미래를 주의 깊게 살펴봐 달라고 부탁했어요.

Mirabel asked Bruno to look into the _____.

Word Box

determined	reveal	future	put ~ together	stair
형 단단히 결심한	통 드러내다	명 미래	~을 끼워 맞추다	명 계단
passageway	time	ripple	living	piece
명 통로	명 시간	통 잔물결처럼 퍼지다	live(살다)의 진행형	명 조각

30 그러면 그것이 금이 가는 것을 멈추고 카시타의 마법을 복구하는 데 도움을 줄 것이라 믿었어요!

She believed it would help stop the cracks and [   ] Casita's magic!

31 손을 잡고 그들은 운이 다한 카시타와 검은 금에 쫓기는 가족들, 그리고 혼돈의 한가운데에 있는 미라벨을 보았어요.

Holding hands, they saw a [   ] Casita, the family pursued by dark cracks, and Mirabel standing amidst the chaos.

32 그리고 빛나는 사람의 모습이 보였는데, 바로 이사벨라였어요!

Then a glowing [   ] ... it was ISABELA!

33 "그녀를 안아 주어라, 그러면 길이 보일 것이다." 브루노가 말했어요.

" [   ] her and you will see the way," said Bruno.

34 미라벨은 이사벨라가 짜증 날 정도로 완벽하다고 생각했어요.

Mirabel thought Isabela was annoyingly [   ].

35 하지만 이사벨라는 미라벨에게 말했어요. 자신은 결코 아부엘라가 만족할 만큼 완벽해질 수 없다고 느낀다고요.

But Isabela told her that she always [   ] she could never be perfect enough for Abuela.

36 바로 그때 촛불이 더 밝게 빛났어요!

Just then, the candle's light glowed [   ]!

37 아부엘라 알마는 미라벨이 모든 것에 지장을 줬다며 화냈어요.

Abuela Alma was angry at all that Mirabel had been [   ]ing.

38 그녀는 마법이 사라지기 시작한 것은 미라벨이 재능을 받지 못한 날부터였다고 말했어요.

She told Mirabel that the magic had started [   ] the day she didn't get a gift.

Word Box

restore 통 복구하다	**embrace** 통 껴안다	**figure** 명 사람 모습	**doomed** 형 운이 다한	**perfect** 형 완벽한
brighter 부 더 밝게	**felt** feel(느끼다)의 과거형	**dying** die(사라지다)의 현재분사	**disrupt** 통 지장을 주다, 방해하다	

50

(39) 미라벨은 뜻밖의 사실을 알게 되었어요. 마법이 사라지고 있는 이유는 가족 중 누구도 아부엘라만큼 뛰어나지 않았기 때문이었어요!

Mirabel had a [_____]: The magic was dying because no one in the family was ever good enough for Abuela Alma!

(40) 거대한 금들이 곳곳에 나타났어요! 초는 거의 완전히 녹아 버렸어요.

Giant cracks [_____]ed everywhere! The candle was almost completely melted away.

(41) 가족들이 초를 살리기 위해 달려 갔지만, 그들의 힘은 서서히 사라지고 있었어요.

The family members raced to save the candle, but their powers were [_____].

(42) 카시타는 마지막으로 노력해 미라벨을 안전한 곳에 두었어요. 그리고는 초가 꺼지고 말았어요.

In its last [_____], Casita got Mirabel to safety. Then the candle went out.

(43) 카시타의 마법은 사라져 버렸어요! 카시타는 돌더미와 흙먼지로 허물어졌어요.

All the magic of Casita was gone! Casita had [_____]d into a pile of rubble and dust.

(44) 엔칸토 전체가 흔들렸어요. 모든 것이 혼돈에 빠졌어요.

The [_____] Encanto shook. Everything was in chaos.

(45) 미라벨은 패배감을 느끼고 집을 뛰쳐나갔어요.

Feeling [_____], Mirabel ran away.

(46) 미라벨은 산들을 지나며 헤매 다녔어요.

Mirabel [_____]ed past the mountains.

(47) 아부엘라는 근처의 강기슭에서 미라벨을 찾았어요.

At a nearby [_____], Abuela found her.

(48) 그곳은 엔칸토가 생겨난 곳이었고, 아부엘라의 남편인 아부엘로 페드로가 사라진 곳이기도 했어요.

It was the same place where the Encanto was born and Abuelo Pedro, Abuela's [_____], was lost.

Word Box

revelation	appear	defeated	effort	riverbank
명 뜻밖의 사실, 폭로	통 나타나다	형 패배한	명 노력	명 강기슭
entire	wander	husband	crumble	fading
형 전체의	통 헤매다	명 남편	통 허물어지다	fade(서서히 사라지다)의 진행형

49 아부엘라는 오래 전 그 밤, 그녀가 얼마나 기적을 바랐는지에 대해 말했어요.

Abuela told Mirabel about that night long ago, how she had ◻◻◻◻ed for a miracle.

50 그 초의 밝은 불빛은 나쁜 사람들을 밀어내고, 그녀와 그녀의 세 쌍둥이들을 보호해 주었어요.

The candle's bright light pushed back the bad men, protecting her and her ◻◻◻◻.

51 아부엘로를 잃자, 아부엘라 내면의 무엇인가가 깨져 버렸어요. 그리고 그 어떤 마법의 불꽃도 그녀를 고칠 수 없었어요.

Losing Abuelo broke something inside Abuela that no magic ◻◻◻◻ could ever repair.

52 그날부터, 아부엘라는 만약 가족이 충분히 강하고, 충분히 노력하면 그녀가 그들을 보호할 수 있을 것이라고 생각했어요.

Since that day, Abuela felt that if the family was strong enough and worked hard enough, she could ◻◻◻◻ them.

53 하지만 이제 아부엘라는 깨달았어요. 그녀의 낙담한 마음이 스스로를 두려움 속에 살게 했다는 사실을요.

But now she realized her ◻◻◻◻ heart had made her live in fear.

54 "저희는 할머니 덕분에 기적을 받았던 거군요." 미라벨이 아부엘라에게 말했어요. 이 말로 아부엘라의 기분이 나아졌어요.

"We were given a miracle because of you," Mirabel told Abuela. This made Abuela feel ◻◻◻◻.

55 "내 사랑… 네가 기적이란다." 그녀가 손녀에게 말했어요.

"Mi Vida... you are the ◻◻◻◻," she told her granddaughter.

56 브루노가 강에 도착했어요. 아부엘라는 그를 껴안았어요.

Bruno arrived at the river. Abuela ◻◻◻◻ged him.

57 "제가 뭔가 중요한 걸 놓친 것 같은 기분이 들어요." 브루노가 말했어요.

"I feel like I ◻◻◻◻ed something important," he said.

Word Box

protect	triplets	broken	pray	flame
통 보호하다	명 세 쌍둥이	형 낙담한	통 간절히 바라다	명 불꽃
hug	miracle	better	miss	
통 껴안다	명 기적	형 더 나은	통 놓치다	

58 "가요." 미라벨이 말했어요. 그리고 세 사람은 집으로 향했어요.

"Come on," Mirabel said, and the three of them _____ed home.

59 아무도 그들이 본 것을 믿을 수 없었어요. 아부엘라가 미라벨과 브루노 옆에서 자랑스럽게 걸어오고 있었거든요!

Nobody could believe what they saw: Abuela, proudly walking _____ Mirabel and Bruno!

60 모두가 깨달았어요. 그들을 특별하게 만들었던 것은 그들의 힘이 아니라, 가족 간의 유대, 즉 서로에 대한 사랑이었다는 사실을요.

Everyone realized what made them truly special wasn't their powers, it was their family _____—their love for one another.

61 그들은 카시타를 다시 짓기 위해 힘을 합쳤어요.

They all worked together to _____ Casita.

62 집에 필요한 마지막 한 조각이 남았어요. 문의 손잡이였죠.

There was just one last piece of the house left: the _____.

63 미라벨이 그것을 집에 설치하자… 카시타는 다시 살아났고, 엔칸토의 마법이 복구되었어요.

As Mirabel _____d it in the house... Casita came back to life and the Encanto's magic was restored.

64 가족들의 재능도 다시 살아났고요! 그리고 마침내, 미라벨은 그녀 자신만의 가치와 가족의 사랑을 느꼈답니다.

The family's gifts worked again! And at last, Mirabel felt her OWN _____ and her family's love.

Word Box

head	rebuild	bond	doorknob
통 ~로 향하다	통 다시 짓다	명 유대	명 문의 손잡이
worth	place	alongside	
명 가치	통 설치하다	전 ~옆에	

LUCA

빈칸에 알맞은 단어를 채워 문장을 완성하세요.

1 루카는 바닷속에서 가족과 함께 사는 친절한 바다 괴물이었어요.

Luca was a [_____] sea monster who lived with his family in the ocean.

2 그는 노랑촉수 떼를 몰면서 하루를 보냈어요.

He spent his days [_____]ing a flock of goatfish.

3 루카는 수면 위의 삶을 꿈꿨지만, 육지에 가는 것은 금지되어 있었어요.

Though he dreamed about life above the surface, Luca was forbidden to go on [_____].

4 그의 부모님은 루카에게 인간은 위험하다고 주의를 주었어요.

His parents [_____]ed him that humans were dangerous.

5 어느 날, 루카는 또 다른 어린 바다 괴물인 알베르토를 만났어요.

One day, Luca met Alberto, another [_____] sea monster.

6 알베르토는 새로운 보물을 모으다 우연히 루카의 물고기 모는 지팡이를 가져가게 되었어요.

As Alberto [_____]ed some new treasures, he accidentally took Luca´s shepherding crook.

7 루카는 그를 쫓아 수면까지 올라갔어요!

Luca [_____]d him all the way to the surface!

8 루카와 알베르토가 육지에 도달했을 때, 그들은 인간으로 변신했어요!

When they reached land, Luca and Alberto [_____]ed into humans!

9 루카 주변의 모든 것들은 이상하면서도 놀라웠어요. 알베르토는 루카를 자신의 비밀 은신처로 데려갔어요.

Everything around Luca was strange but amazing. Then Alberto took Luca to his [_____].

Word Box

land	young	friendly	warn	herd
뗑 육지, 땅	혱 어린	혱 친절한	통 주의를 주다	통 (짐승을) 몰다
collect	hideout	transform	chase	
통 모으다, 수집하다	뗑 비밀 은신처	통 바뀌다, 변형시키다	통 뒤쫓다	

54

10 그곳은 인간들의 멋진 물건으로 가득 차 있었는데, 베스파 스쿠터의 포스터도 있었어요. 루카는 마음을 뺏겨버렸어요.

It was full of [_____] human things, including a poster of a shiny Vespa. Luca was fascinated.

11 주위를 살핀 루카는 그들만의 베스파 스쿠터를 만들 수 있겠다고 생각했어요! 소년들은 당장 일을 시작했어요.

Looking around, he realized they could [_____] their own Vespa! The boys got to work right away.

12 루카와 알베르토는 매일 그 섬에서 온갖 종류의 베스파 스쿠터를 만들었어요. 그들이 찾아낸 모든 것들로요.

Every day on the island, Luca and Alberto made all [_____]s of Vespas with anything they could find.

13 그들은 심지어 한 대를 같이 타고는 공중으로 날아오르기까지 했어요!

They even rode one together and soared through the [_____]!

14 루카는 지금까지 그렇게 재미있게 놀아 본 적이 없었답니다. 하지만 루카의 부모님은 걱정이 되었어요.

Luca had never had so much [_____]. But Luca's parents were worried.

15 그들은 루카가 삼촌과 함께 깊은 바닷속에 사는 것이 더 안전할 것이라 결정했어요.

They decided Luca would be [_____] living deep in the ocean with his uncle.

16 부모님이 그를 멀리 보내기 전에, 루카는 알베르토를 찾아 떠났어요.

Before they could [_____] him away, Luca left to find Alberto.

17 루카와 알베르토는 포르토로소라는 해안 도시로 헤엄쳐 갔어요. 그곳에서 줄리아라는 이름의 인간 소녀를 만났어요.

Luca and Alberto swam to the [_____] town of Portorosso, where they met a human girl named Giulia.

18 그녀는 처음에 소년들을 의심했지만, 포르토로소 컵이라고 불리는 지역 경주의 팀원에 그들이 완벽하다는 것을 깨달았어요.

She was [_____] about the boys at first, but she soon realized that they would be perfect teammates for a local race called the Portorosso Cup.

Word Box

air	build	fun	neat	kind
명 공중	동 만들어 내다	명 재미	형 멋진, 정돈된	명 종류
unsure	send	seaside	safer	
형 의심스러워하는	동 보내다	형 해안의	형 더 안전한	

19 상금이 있으면 진짜 베스파 스쿠터를 살 수 있고, 그러면 그들은 어디든 갈 수 있을 거예요!

With the [ ] money, they could buy a real Vespa——and then they could go anywhere!

20 소년들은 줄리아의 아빠인 마시모를 만났는데 그는 어부였어요.

The boys met Giulia's dad, Massimo, who was a [ ].

21 그들은 경주 참가비를 받는 대신 마시모의 일을 돕기로 했어요.

They agreed to work for him in exchange for the race's entry [ ].

22 마시모의 고양이인 마키아벨리는 소년들을 주의 깊게 감시했어요. 수상한 냄새를 맡았거든요!

Massimo's cat, Machiavelli, kept a close eye on the boys. He smelled something [ ]!

23 루카와 알베르토는 우승이 쉽지 않을 것이라 생각했어요. 경주에서 다섯 번이나 우승한 에르콜레도 참가하거든요.

Luca and Alberto knew that winning wasn't going to be easy. Ercole, the five-time race [ ], was also competing.

24 그 악당은 세 친구를 비웃으며, 맹세코 그들을 패배시키겠다고 했어요.

The bully [ ]ed the three friends and vowed to defeat them.

25 루카 팀은 어느 때보다도 마음을 단단히 먹고, 포르토로소 컵의 세 가지 경기를 대비하기 위해 훈련을 시작했어요.

More [ ] than ever, the team began training for the three events of the Portorosso Cup.

26 줄리아는 수영을 연습했어요. 알베르토는 파스타 먹기를 연습했어요. 그리고 루카는 자전거 타기를 연습했어요.

Giulia [ ]d swimming. Alberto practiced eating pasta. And Luca practiced riding a bike.

27 시간이 흐르면서 그들은 사이 좋은 친구가 되었어요.

Over time, they [ ] good friends.

Word Box

champion	fisherman	entry fee	prize money	fishy
명 선수권 대회 우승자	명 어부	명 참가비	명 상금	형 수상한
taunt	practice	determined	became	
동 비웃다	동 연습하다	형 단단히 결심한	become(~이 되다)의 과거형	

56

28 줄리아와 루카는 읽고 배우는 것을 무척 좋아했어요. 루카는 줄리아가 학교에 다닌다는 사실이 놀라웠어요.
그도 가고 싶어졌어요!

Giulia and Luca loved to read and learn. Luca was [_____] that Giulia went to school. He wanted to go, too!

29 알베르토는 소외감을 느끼기 시작했어요. 그는 루카가 줄리아와 함께 학교에 가는 것을 원하지 않았기 때문에, 자신이 바다 괴물임을 드러냈어요!

Alberto began to feel left out. He didn't want Luca to go to school with Giulia, so he [_____]ed that he was a sea monster!

30 줄리아는 충격을 받았지만, 루카는 계속 조용하게 있었어요.

Giulia was shocked, but Luca stayed [_____].

31 소란을 들은 에르콜레는 달려와서 작살을 던졌어요. 알베르토는 제때 도망쳤어요.

Hearing the commotion, Ercole ran up and threw his [_____]. Alberto escaped just in time.

32 곧 줄리아는 루카도 바다 괴물이라는 사실을 알게 됐어요.

Giulia soon [_____]d out that Luca was a sea monster, too.

33 그녀는 누군가 그에 관한 사실을 알게 된다면 루카가 위험해질 것 같아 걱정됐어요.

She was worried that Luca would be in [_____] if anyone knew the truth about him.

34 나중에 루카는 알베르토를 찾아냈어요. 알베르토는 루카에게 화가 나서 더 이상 경주에 참가하고 싶지 않았어요.

Later, Luca found Alberto. He was angry at Luca and didn't want to [_____] anymore.

35 하지만 루카는 포기하지 않았어요. 그는 친구들에게 베스파를 사다주기로 약속했어요.

But Luca wouldn't [_____] [_____]. He promised to get them a Vespa.

Word Box

amazed	harpoon	quiet	give up
형 놀란	명 작살	형 조용한	포기하다
race	**danger**	**figure out**	**reveal**
통 경주하다, 참가하다	명 위험	알아내다	통 드러내다

36 마침내 포르토로소 컵이 열리는 날이 다가왔어요. 루카는 줄리아를 보호하기 위해 혼자서만 출전하기로 결심했어요.

Finally, the day of the Portorosso Cup arrived. Luca decided to race alone to
[   ] Giulia.

37 바다 괴물이라는 그의 정체를 숨기는 것은 아슬아슬한 일이었어요.

It was risky to hide his sea monster [   ].

38 첫 번째 경기 동안, 그는 물속에서 변신하는 것을 막기 위해 잠수복을 입었어요.

During the first event, he wore a diving suit to [   ] transforming in the water.

39 이어서 루카는 파스타 먹기 시합도 끝마쳤어요.

Next, he [   ]d the pasta-eating competition.

40 자전거 경주 동안, 루카는 다른 선수들을 왼쪽, 오른쪽으로 지나치며 아주 빨리 앞으로 달려나갔어요.

During the bike race, Luca [   ]ed ahead, passing racers left and right.

41 루카는 자신을 찾아다니던 부모님과 마주쳤어요. 하지만 루카는 페달을 있는 힘껏 계속 밟았어요.

He ran into his parents, who had been searching for him.
But Luca kept [   ]ing as hard as he could.

42 비가 오기 시작했어요.

It began to [   ].

43 알베르토가 루카를 돕기 위해 도착했지만, 곤경에 빠졌어요. 비 때문에 알베르토가 바다 괴물로 변한 거예요!

Alberto arrived to help Luca, but he got into [   ]: the rain transformed him into a sea monster!

44 사람들이 알베르토를 그물에 가두었어요.

A crowd trapped Alberto in a [   ].

45 루카는 빗속을 뚫고 달려가 친구를 구조했어요.

Luca rode into the rain and [   ]d his friend.

Word Box

avoid	zoom	protect	complete	identity
통 막다, 피하다	통 아주 빨리 가다	통 보호하다	통 끝마치다	명 정체
pedal	**net**	**trouble**	**rain**	**rescue**
통 페달을 밟다	명 그물	명 곤경	통 비가 오다	통 구조하다

58

46 이제 모든 사람들이 루카도 바다 괴물이라는 것을 알게 됐어요! 에르콜레가 쫓아왔기 때문에 두 소년들은 도망쳤어요.

Now everyone _____ Luca was a sea monster, too! The boys raced away as Ercole chased them.

47 에르콜레가 작살을 겨누기 전에, 줄리아가 자전거를 타고 달려가 그에게 부딪쳤어요!

Before Ercole could take aim with his harpoon, Giulia _____ed her bike into him!

48 루카와 알베르토는 다친 줄리아를 보고는 끼익 소리를 내며 자전거를 멈췄어요.

Seeing their injured friend, Luca and Alberto came to a screeching _____.

49 그들은 자전거에서 내려 줄리아 옆으로 급히 달려갔어요.

They climbed off their bike and _____ed to Giulia's side.

50 루카와 알베르토는 사람들이 자신들을 쳐다보고 있어서 긴장되었어요.

Luca and Alberto were _____ as the crowd watched them.

51 도움을 주겠다고 가장 먼저 나선 사람은 마시모였어요.

Massimo was the first to step _____.

52 모두가 놀랍게도, 마시모는 소년들을 있는 그대로 받아들였어요.

To everyone's surprise, he _____ed the boys as they were.

53 그리고 그는 중요한 사실을 지적했어요. 루카와 알베르토가 결승선을 막 지나 자전거를 세웠다는 사실을요. 그들이 그 경주에서 우승한 거예요!

And he _____ed out something important: Luca and Alberto had stopped their bike just past the finish line. They had won the race!

54 그날 저녁, 루카와 알베르토는 마침내 그들만의 베스파 스쿠터를 샀어요. 그리고 그들은 마시모의 뒷마당에 모여 식사를 했어요.

Later that evening, Luca and Alberto finally _____ their very own Vespa, and the group gathered in Massimo's backyard to share a meal.

Word Box

knew know(알게 되다)의 과거형	halt 몡 멈춤	crash 동 부딪치다	rush 동 급히 움직이다	nervous 형 긴장한
bought buy(사다)의 과거형	accept 동 받아들이다	point out 지적하다	step forward 도움을 주겠다고 나서다	

55 루카의 가족은 큰 환영을 받았어요.

Luca's family was [   ]d with open arms.

56 학교에 가기 위해 줄리아가 떠날 때가 됐어요. 하지만 학교에 가는 사람은 그녀만이 아니었어요.

It was soon [   ] for Giulia to go away to school. But she wasn't the only one.

57 알베르토는 루카의 부모님께 말하고 베스파를 팔아서 깜짝 선물로 기차표를 샀어요. 루카도 학교에 가게 되었어요!

As a surprise, Alberto had talked to Luca's parents, [   ] the Vespa, and bought a train ticket. Luca would be going to school!

58 루카는 알베르토도 같이 가길 바랐지만, 알베르토는 마시모와 함께 포르토로소에 머무를 계획이었어요.

Luca wanted his friend to come with him, but Alberto [   ]ed to stay in Portorosso with Massimo.

59 비록 그들은 떨어져 있지만 여름의 추억과 그들의 우정은 영원히 지속될 것을 알았어요.

Even if they were apart, they knew their summer memories——and their friendship—— would [   ] forever.

60

DISNEY · PIXAR
Story Collection 2

Practice Book

Part 1 **단어 연습 (Word Practice)**

스토리북에 등장한 핵심 어휘를 익힙니다. 어려운 단어들을 순서대로 정리해 보고,
이 외에도 잘 모르는 단어는 사전에서 찾아 뜻과 철자를 기록합니다.

Part 2 **전체 문장 연습 (Sentence Practice)**

읽은 내용을 다시 떠올리며 우리말에 맞도록 문장을 완성합니다.
빈칸에 들어갈 알맞은 단어를 찾는 과정에서 문장 구조와 표현을 익힐 수 있습니다.